With special best wishes

for love, happiness and

world peace.

Many Blessings

[signature]

Azim's Bardo

A Father's Journey from
Murder to Forgiveness

by Azim Khamisa
with Carl Goldman

Rising Star Press
Los Altos, California

Azim's Bardo

Rising Star Press
Los Altos, California

Library of Congress Catalog Card Number: 98-66932

Interior design and copyediting by Joanne Shwed, Backspace Ink, Pacifica, CA

Jacket design by Rudy Marinacci, The Bookmill, Saratoga, CA

Cover art reprinted with the generous permission of *San Diego Magazine*. Copyright © 1996, San Diego Magazine Publishing Company, San Diego, CA. Originally used for the cover story of the January 1996 issue. The eyes are those of Azim Khamisa.

Manufactured in the United States of America

Publisher's Cataloging-in-Publication
(Provided by Quality Books, Inc.)

Khamisa, Azim.
    Azim's bardo : a father's journey from murder to forgiveness / by Azim Khamisa ; with Carl Goldman. -- 1st ed.
    p. cm.
    Preassigned LCCN: 98-66932
    ISBN: 0-933670-02-8

    1. Juvenile homicide--California--San Diego County--Case studies. 2. Khamisa, Azim. 3. Fathers of murder victims--California--San Diego County--Biography. 4. Criminal justice, Administration of. 5. Khamisa, Tariq. I. Title.

HV9067. H6K53 1998   364.15'23'0979498
                                      QBI98-801

To my son, Tariq,
    for connecting me with my heart and soul

To my daughter, Tasreen,
    for keeping that connection alive

Bringing this book to completion required help from a host of people, and I give my most heartfelt thanks.

———————

To Tariq's mother Almas, for her support and friendship.

To my daughter Tasreen, for having joined me and her brother's Foundation in the crusade against youth violence.

To my family for their love during our time of crisis, and always:
    Dad, Mum
    My sister Neyleen
    My brother Nazir, his wife Shelina, and their daughter
        Soraiya
    My sister Yasmin, her husband Tony and their sons
        Karim, Nazim, and Salim

To Nargis, for the inspiration she has given me.

To Dan Pearson, for standing by me as a brother.

To Kit Goldman, for all she does for me, my family, and the Tariq Khamisa Foundation.

To Brian Horsley, for his many significant contributions to the Foundation's work.

To Ples Felix, for becoming my new friend, joining our cause, and writing the afterword to this book.

To Peter Deddeh, for compassionate guidance through the criminal justice process, and for writing the foreword to this book.

To Rashida Hunzai, for whose scholarly knowledge of our Ismaili faith and resource material for this book I am deeply grateful.

To Nizar and Yasmin Teja, for their friendship, partnership, and resourcefulness.

To Alan Luckhurst, Kim Cromwell, Nazim Karim, and my aunt, Gulshan Ahmed, for their incisive draft review comments.

To the advisory board and steering committee of the Tariq Khamisa Foundation, for their countless volunteer hours and wise leadership.

To all those who have supported the Foundation's work by generously donating their time and other resources.

To Ginger Bate, for her thorough and helpful editorial review of the entire manuscript.

And finally, to my collaborator, Carl Goldman, for the compassion and energy he brought to this project.

bardo *n.* (Tibetan) A transition or gap between the completion of one situation and the onset of another. From *bar*—"in between"—and *do*— "suspended" or "thrown."

Sogyal Rinpoche,
The Tibetan Book of Living and Dying
HarperSanFrancisco, 1993

Contents

Foreword

On January 21, 1995, Tony Edward Hicks murdered Tariq Khamisa. Criminal charges were filed against Hicks six days later. As the prosecutor representing the San Diego County District Attorney's Office, I realized immediately that this case would be unique and emotionally charged.

Hicks was only 14 years and 3 months old. On January 27, 1995, he became the youngest person in the history of California to face adult criminal charges.

Prior to January 1, 1995, juveniles under 16 years old could not be tried as adults in California. Amid a rising juvenile crime rate, California passed legislation which allowed adult court treatment for 14- and 15-year-olds who committed certain specified crimes. Tony Hicks was the first juvenile to feel the brunt of the new law.

In seeking to have Hicks tried as an adult, newly elected District Attorney Paul Pfingst had to make the first controversial decision of his young administration. Pfingst had campaigned on a platform promising to get tough on violent juvenile crime; he believed that people who kill in the course of a robbery attempt should be sent to adult court.

That decision propelled the case into the intense glare of the local media. The glare was magnified by the many concerns this incident raised: guns in the hands of children; neighborhood gangs; a victim "just doing a job" when he was shot down; a relatively middle-class neighborhood thrust into the uncomfortable limelight of violence. Shock waves went through the community.

Highly emotional public debate sprang up on whether 14-year-olds belonged in adult court under any circumstances. A torrent of stories, editorials and letters to the editor appeared in local newspapers. Radio talk shows and television news programs featured the crime. When I gave presentations to civic groups or schools, someone would invariably ask about it. Even today, over three years after the murder, people vividly remember this incident. In my 15-year prosecutorial career, only a handful of cases have garnered so much visibility.

During interviews, at speaking engagements—even on social occasions—the question I was always asked was: "How do you feel about trying to send this young man to adult court?" The issue was a troubling, complex one for me. I pictured Tariq slumped in his car, a father losing his son forever, a mother and sister in perpetual mourning. I hoped our decision would eventually lead to justice, deter others from committing such horrific crimes, and bring some closure for the Khamisa family.

But it is certainly not a proud day when a society has to prosecute its 14-year-olds as adults.

The District Attorney's decision to move toward an adult trial had to be confirmed by a court. The law says a judge must hold a hearing to determine whether a minor is "fit" or "unfit" for the juvenile system. If Hicks were found fit for juvenile court, his maximum penalty would be confinement in the California Youth Authority until his 25th birthday. In stark contrast, if convicted of first-degree murder as an adult, he would face a state prison term of 25 years to life. On May 4, 1995, Superior

Court Judge Federico Castro found Tony Hicks "unfit" for juvenile treatment, and remanded him to adult court.

I met Tariq Khamisa's father, Azim, for the first time while the fitness hearing was in progress. I was immediately taken by his gentle and composed manner. Families of murder victims are often understandably bitter and suspicious. Though suffering greatly, his demeanor showed none of that.

I was planning to brief Azim on the details of the court proceedings, but he was clearly focused on bigger issues. While describing the abject devastation caused by the killing of his son, Azim said he felt that both Tariq and Tony were victims. He decried how our society could tolerate children killing children. He went on to say that he bore Tony Hicks no ill will.

This absolutely astounded me. I had never encountered such a reflective and compassionate family member in a murder case.

At subsequent meetings, Azim and I brainstormed about some of the problems that create societal victims: teen pregnancy, drug use, gangs. He told me that he and friends and business associates were considering starting a foundation to address those concerns. The foundation would be named for Tariq.

Azim believed he had benefited greatly from this country's bounty, but that his individual pursuit of material success had allowed him to overlook social ills. Now he had been profoundly affected by those ills. He could overlook them no longer.

Although crushed by his son's death, Azim decided to focus on attacking the problems that create youngsters who kill. He would honor the memory of his slain son by working to break the cycle of youth violence.

During the month-long fitness hearing to determine if Tony Hicks would be tried as a juvenile or an adult, Hicks' grandfather,

Ples Felix, sat in pained silence as he listened to the details of his grandson's tragic life. The dignity with which he conducted himself, and the support he gave to his grandson, impressed me greatly. He would later impress me even more.

An extraordinary story told in this book is the bond which developed between Azim Khamisa and Ples Felix. It is a match unprecedented in my experience: a partnership of men brought together by murder, now joined by their determination to combat youth violence. Ples has pledged his support for the Tariq Khamisa Foundation, and is a member of its advisory board.

I believe the relationship between Azim Khamisa and Ples Felix will resonate throughout the country, as it did with me.

Every parent's nightmare is a phone ringing in the night . . . a police officer on the line . . . a conversation that begins, "I'm sorry, but your child has . . ." My job has required me to listen to chilling tales of those phone calls all too often. I hope others will join Azim in his goal to shield parents from having to answer that terrible call.

The story of the youngest adult court-bound criminal in California legal history, and the father of the young man he killed, started in tragedy. Azim Khamisa and the remarkable people working with him have shown us how the power of the human spirit can turn tragedy into a story of grace and restoration.

Peter Deddeh
Deputy District Attorney, San Diego, California
March 1998

Tariq Khamisa
1974–1995

Murder

This is the Hour of Lead—
Remembered, if outlived,
As Freezing persons, recollect the Snow—
First—Chill—then Stupor—then the letting go—

Emily Dickinson, *The Complete Poems,* no. 341

On the night of January 21, 1995, an emotional nuclear bomb dropped on my life. My only son, Tariq—a 20-year-old student at San Diego State University—was shot and killed while delivering pizzas for an Italian restaurant in San Diego. His killer belonged to a street gang called the Black Mob.

The killer had a baby face because he wasn't old enough to have outgrown one. He was 14 years old.

Earlier that night, I had flown back to San Diego from Mexico City in a volatile, mixed-mood state. On the good side, my recent efforts as an international investment banker were paying off: the business deal I had been putting together in Mexico looked like a winner. Also, I had been informed that my father's open heart surgery two nights before appeared successful. And finally, I am always exhilarated when returning to the beautiful city of San Diego, a place I feel lucky to call home.

The bad news was that I had that lump-of-lead-where-your heart-should-be feeling we all get when romance dies. Earlier in the week, Mirtila, the beautiful Mexican woman I loved, ended our relationship. I needed warm, sympathetic friendship to help me weather this blow, and I knew it would be waiting. My best friend, Dan Pearson, and his wife, Kit Goldman, were picking me up at the airport. We were going to a party, and I was looking forward to a little homecoming celebration.

Dan is special. We feel we must have been brothers in earlier lives. I had no idea how much I would soon be leaning on him for strength.

After the party, Kit, Dan and I migrated to my home in the San Diego suburb of La Jolla. We relaxed and brought each other up to date, warm cognac providing a delightful counterpoint to the cool winter night outside. They left just past midnight, and I headed upstairs to bed. I had that feeling of deep exhaustion that sets the stage for a great night's sleep. Another action-packed business trip successfully completed, topped off by a lovely evening.

As I drifted off, I had no way of knowing this would be the last good night's sleep I would have for a hellishly long time. I had no way of knowing that January 21, 1995 marked the end of the life I had known, and that January 22 would usher in a terrifying new era. I had no way of knowing that in the section of San Diego known as North Park, 12 miles south of where I lay in my bed, my son lay dead, his feet sticking grotesquely out of the faded Volkswagen in which he'd been shot.

———

As I slept, the strands of the fabric to be woven by Tariq's death were beginning to enwrap others.

Sal Giacalone, co-owner of DiMille's, the Italian restaurant to which the fatal pizza order had been called in, was having a quiet dinner at home with his family when the phone rang. A hysterical employee gave him what seemed like an impossible piece of news: Tariq, well liked, on the job for only two months, had been shot dead during a delivery. Sal put down the phone and rushed to the restaurant. The truth began to sink in quickly: homicide detectives got there at the same time he did.

Sal entered his restaurant. The phone jangled to life, and he picked it up. Jennifer Patchen, Tariq's fiancée, was on the line. Tariq should have been home already, and she was worried. Was he there?

Unsure of the facts, Sal didn't tell Jennifer the terrible truth. "I'll have him call you when he gets in," he said. Later, again and again through that long night, Jennifer called the restaurant. On the advice of the police, no one picked up the phone. Sal says that the sound of the phone, ringing, ringing and ringing, will haunt him for the rest of his life.

––––––––––

Not far from where police cars and barricades surrounded Tariq's car, a man named Ples Felix turned off his television set with an uneasy feeling. Watching the late news, he had been stunned to see that a pizza delivery man had been killed close to where he lived with his 14-year-old grandson.

Under normal circumstances, Ples and I would never have met. But the lines of fate had been cast; our lives were destined to be entwined.

––––––––––

I got up Sunday morning feeling refreshed. Around 8:30, my housekeeper showed up to start restoring order to my bachelor townhouse. I let her in, and she handed me a business card that she found tucked in the screen door. The card contained an ominous-sounding official title: Sergeant Lampert. San Diego Police. Homicide Division. On the back was a handwritten note: "We are trying to reach Tariq Khamisa's family."

The full significance of the "Homicide Division" on the card didn't register at first. Police. My son could be a bit hot-headed. Maybe he'd gotten into a fight, maybe even arrested. I called the number on the card, and asked for Sergeant Lampert.

The woman who answered said she wasn't in. I gave her my name and told her I had received a message to call this office. There was a pause.

"I'm sorry," she said. "Tariq Khamisa was shot and killed last night."

Reality did a fade. Not possible! Not believable! Could not be! My insides began to churn in a mixture of shock and rejection. I picked up the phone again and frantically dialed Tariq's number. Jennifer answered. She was in tears. When I heard her voice, I knew.

She had known since 4 AM.

Sobbing, she said the police had come to see her and given her the stark facts. A delivery order for two large pizzas had been phoned into DiMille's shortly before closing time. A bogus apartment address had been given. It had been a robbery setup—a "pizza jacking," in street slang. It would have been Tariq's last delivery of the night. It was the last delivery—the last anything—of his young life.

I felt my own life spirit draining away. My thoughts spun incoherently, and a flood of horrible emotion washed over me. I was drowning in grief and loss. But thoughts of the other people in Tariq's life pushed through the pain: Almas, Tariq's mother.

My daughter Tasreen, Tariq's older sister. They had to be told. How do you tell a mother her son is dead? How do you tell a sister her brother is gone forever?

From what seemed like a different universe, I remembered that Almas was visiting relatives in Vancouver, and that Tasreen was with her. Almas and I had remained good friends after our divorce in 1981. We usually know where the other can be reached. I managed to dial the number. The phone was answered by Altaf, one of Almas' brothers. "I have to speak to Almas," I managed to choke out. "Something terrible has happened."

When Almas came on the line, all I could do was blurt it out. "Tariq has been shot. He is dead."

"NO! NO! NO!" she choked out, in disbelief and shock. Her piercing shriek will stay with me forever. I heard her phone hit the floor.

"As the reality sank in, I couldn't stand on my feet," she recalled later. "It was as if my legs would not support me. I fell to my knees, screaming with shock and crying hysterically. My mother was trying to find out from me what had happened, and it took forever to tell her. All I could say was, 'Tariq, Tariq, Tariq,' but I couldn't utter the words that he was dead. Things were a blur after that. All I remember is the phone ringing constantly, relatives beginning to arrive, and my brother trying to get me on the first available flight to San Diego."

Altaf came back on the line. I stumbled through relating the few facts I knew. Then I realized I had to call my mother and give her the tragic news. Usually delighted to hear my voice, this time she would not be. Her grandson was gone.

"How will we tell your father?" Mom cried out hysterically when I told her. Dad was still in serious condition from the extensive heart surgery. Seven years earlier he had undergone a

*From left: Tariq's mother Almas,
sister Tasreen, and aunt Neyleen*

quadruple bypass. Three days ago, in a 12½-hour operation, surgeons repaired the first four, then did three more bypasses. The operation had been successful, but his health remained precarious. We were worried that the shock of Tariq's death could be a death sentence for him as well.

My daughter, Tasreen, was with my mother that night. My telephone call is burned into her memory. "My grandmother picked up the phone and started screaming," she remembers. "I never heard anyone scream like that. My first thought was that something had happened to my grandfather. But I couldn't understand why, because we had seen him the night before, and he was eating a steak dinner, and he was fine. And then my grandmother handed me the phone. Everything got kind of blurry then. I think I started screaming, too."

We decided it was too risky to tell Dad. Mom would stay in close touch with his doctors to figure out when the time was right. Until then, everyone around him would try to act as though nothing had happened.

I talked with Mom for half an hour. We comforted each other, drawing on the love we shared, trying not to be swallowed up by the grief, almost clinging to each other through the telephone wires, unwilling to hang up and break the connection.

Finally, we said goodbye. I slowly put the phone back in its cradle. I sat still. My home was silent. Empty. Unbearable.

I picked up the phone again and called Kit and Dan. Kit answered. For the third time, I told the news of my son's death. Her scream, "Tariq's been shot . . . killed . . . murdered!" jarred Dan from the middle of a meditation. He picked up the extension in their bedroom. I said the next thing that came to mind: "My life has ended."

"Don't do anything," they said. "We'll be right over."

Above: Azim, Dan Pearson and Kit Goldman.

Left: Tariq and his fianceé, Jennifer.

Later, Dan talked about the drive to my house.

"I had a real concern that Azim might not pull through," he recalled. "I was terrified for him—and for myself, because he was so close to me, and I was so close to him. I dreaded it. I dreaded for both of us. For all three of us."

I waited for them in a lightless emotional abyss. I paced. I mumbled incoherently. The phone rang. My younger brother Nazir was taking the next plane to San Diego from his home in Seattle. My feet dragged me across the floor of my home in random, meaningless patterns. I pulled my hair. The phone rang. It was my mother, urging me to "Keep saying Salwat." Salwat is an Islamic chant we recite at times of extreme difficulty or catastrophe: *Oh Allah! Shower thy blessings on [Prophet] Muhammad and his progeny.* "We are praying for you," she said.

I had been alone in my home for an eternity before Kit and Dan arrived. It was less than an hour. We embraced standing, holding each other up. Strength returned. My "older brother" was with me. Kit left me with Dan and went to get Tariq's fiancée, Jennifer, so she could be with us also.

I had met Jennifer several times, but didn't know her well. She and Tariq were the same age (20), went to the same college (San Diego State), and shared the same major (art). They had been together for a year, engaged for two months.

Jennifer gave us more detail on Tariq's final hours. On his way to deliver the fatal order to the Louisiana Street address, Tariq had stopped by their apartment. He told her he had one last delivery to make, but wanted to see her briefly first. He brought her a soft drink. Then he left.

Jennifer said witnesses had seen four teenagers running from the scene of the slaying. As we listened, I saw anger growing in Dan, a man who has studied and practiced Eastern religious philosophies of peace, love and forgiveness for over 20 years. He reads from the Bhagavad-Gita, a sacred Hindu text, every day. Later, when we were alone, Dan said, "I hope they catch those little bastards and fry them."

His statement, and its force, made me take an instant look inside myself. Almost to my surprise, I discovered that what Dan felt was not what I felt. My grief, my consciousness of irreparable loss, was overwhelming. But the emotion of vengeance was not part of the internal jumble I perceived. A phrase came to mind, a phrase that was to stay with me, and become a key part of the new direction of my life: "There were victims on both ends of that gun."

For the next few hours the phone rang constantly. Family and friends from Kenya, Uganda, England and Canada were getting the news. Finally, I couldn't talk anymore. Kit and Dan fielded the calls. With their voices in the background, my mind whirled: I was Tariq's father. Aren't fathers supposed to protect their children and make everything all right? Shouldn't I have been able to keep my son safe and secure if I had done the right things? I was overcome with helplessness.

Two homicide detectives arrived to begin their investigation. They assured me they were doing everything they could to find Tariq's killers. An autopsy was in progress. They asked for a recent photograph of Tariq, and left.

As afternoon faded to evening, the cars and airplane flights of family and friends began to arrive. ("The longest flight of my life," Tasreen remembers.) Incredible to think that less than 24 hours ago my own flight had been vectoring into San Diego International airport, my mind filled with anticipation of an enjoyable homecoming evening.

The house filled with loving faces and friendly voices. I needed them badly. I turned to my brother Nazir for emotional support. That night he was the elder, and I the younger.

We had to decide how we were going to handle the media. Newspaper and television reporters wanted statements from the family. We decided that Nazir and my friend Ward Leber, CEO of the Child Safety Network Trust, would act as our spokesmen.

During his discussions with reporters, Nazir could not help confronting the human need to make sense out of the insensible, to understand the incomprehensible. "Why, why has this happened to Tariq?" he pleaded, his voice as shaky as his legs. "We need to know a reason."

Ward gave television reporters the toll-free number of the Child Safety Network Trust. He encouraged anyone who might have information concerning Tariq's murder to call the hot line. We didn't realize at that moment just how important this was: Ward and his hot line would end up providing the key link to the murderers' identities.

In addition to friends and family, members of the Ismaili mosque I belong to streamed in through the afternoon and evening. (Ismailis are members of the Islamic faith. The word "Islam" has many meanings including "peace," "greeting," "safety," "submission," and "salvation.") They brought curries, rice, meat and vegetable dishes, hugs, prayers and support. My community was responding in my time of need.

As each person or group arrived, they wanted to know the details. When tragedy strikes, humans seem to have an insatiable need for information and explanation. We told and retold what we knew of Tariq's fate. But with each arrival, each retelling, I felt myself becoming more paralyzed by the emotional maelstrom.

A family party in happier times.
From left: Azim, sister Neyleen, parents Remy and
Noordin, sister Yasmin, and brother Nazir.

All through that night, each of us clung to our faith and to each other. Kit and Dan left at one in the morning, as they had under such vastly different circumstances the morning before. Everyone went off to bed. I was exhausted, yet sleep was impossible. This nightmare didn't need sleep to exist . . . it was real. And it was just beginning.

―――――――

Tariq's memorial service was held Tuesday night. Kit, a veteran theatrical producer, had miraculously been able to arrange everything—program, music, speakers, and a location—in one day. It was raining outside, fitting accompaniment to our tears inside. Two hundred and fifty people came together on that rainy night to help us send Tariq on the next part of his journey.

"Tariq Khamisa touched more lives in his 20 years than most people do in a lifetime," Kit eulogized in her opening tribute. "By his very nature, Tariq inspired others to feel connected, worthy, optimistic and kindhearted."

Tasreen composed a farewell to her brother, and a friend read it aloud: "I feel so fortunate and blessed to have been his sister," she wrote. "There are no words to describe the feeling I have for him, and the pain I feel for our loss. My life will never be the same again."

Other friends and family members spoke or read poems and selections from religious and spiritual books. A young man from our mosque—like Tariq, a San Diego State University student—chanted the Fathiha, an Islamic prayer in honor of the dead.

Like Tasreen, Jennifer was too grief-stricken to speak herself. A family friend, Barcy, delivered her eulogy for her. Over the last five months of his life Tariq had kept a journal, and Barcy read from one of the entries:

Today I took control of my life. I can no longer blame others for my mistakes. I am responsible for my actions. No one is perfect—I don't want to be perfect. I know that I don't know. That's all I need to know.

Barcy continued with Jennifer's eulogy, voicing her positive, uplifting spiritual view: "Although Tariq's body was young, his soul was very old. Somehow I know he made everything right in his life before he left us. Saturday night, January 21, 1995, was a *good* day for Tariq to die."

I can no longer blame others, my son had written. Even in my grief, I felt the impact of his wisdom and the strength of his direction. These words were destined to stay with me.

————

The morning after Tariq's memorial, we flew to Vancouver, where he was to be buried.

At the time of his death, I had been reading a book Mirtila had given me: *The Tibetan Book of Living and Dying*. I brought it to read on the plane. My relationship with Mirtila was over, but I suddenly realized that one seed it had planted would continue to grow.

I thought Mirtila was obsessed with death, and had told her so. "I *am* obsessed with death," she explained, "because I want to understand it, so I can live a fuller life." Now it was I who had to understand death, and come to terms with it, so I could return to life.

I believe Mirtila was sent into my life to prepare me to start understanding death.

A chapter in *The Tibetan Book of Living and Dying* discusses the Tibetan Buddhist concept of a "bardo." The word describes a transitional state. "Bar" means "in between," and "do" means "suspended" or "thrown." Death is the most extreme bardo, but between birth and death we experience other bardos. Buddhists believe bardos represent times of opportunity: if you have prepared yourself with the wisdom of the masters, your soul can make a quantum leap in its quest for enlightenment.

Jennifer's memorial eulogy reverberated in my mind. I realized Tariq's soul had reached its most challenging bardo—at least so far. Somehow, he had managed to philosophically prepare himself. His soul was ready to move to greater enlightenment.

And I, too, was entering my most significant bardo. The quality of the rest of my life would hinge on how I handled this tragedy. Above the drone of the jet's engines, I began to read aloud to Tasreen and Jennifer from *The Tibetan Book of Living and Dying*.

Tariq had been dead for four days, and my father had still not been told. Keeping up the pretense was tearing up my family, but the doctors strongly advised against giving him the news. He remained in serious condition. They wanted him kept calm, fearing that anything which upset him would be dangerous to his recovery. But not telling him meant we were depriving him of his right to attend his grandson's funeral. Disease and operations are not the only things dangerous to hearts.

We agonized over this decision. There was no risk-free approach. Finally, we decided that Dad's right to know had to prevail. If he felt he was able to be with the family at the funeral, we had no right to deny him. The surgery might heal; the broken heart might not. It fell to my older sister Yasmin to tell him.

Dad had been sedated. Yasmin told him gently she had some bad news. They held hands and prayed. When she finally told him, he didn't understand at first. "Is Tariq in the hospital?" he asked. "No," Yasmin answered quietly. "He didn't make it. He died at the scene."

After the first shock, Dad broke down and cried. Hugging him, Yasmin told him the funeral was the next day. The doctors had said he could go, for a short time, in a wheelchair. It was his decision. "Of course I have to be there," he cried.

Yasmin's tender, careful touch in this incredibly difficult and sensitive situation probably saved our family the loss of another precious life.

———————

Tariq's funeral was Thursday morning. Vancouver was wet and cold. The mosque was full. Tariq lay on the ground, wrapped in a white shroud, only his face visible. Almas, Tasreen and I stood before him. Then I knelt on the floor beside my son's body and kissed him, as 1,400 people paid their final respects in the custom of the Ismaili faith.

There is no formal seating in a mosque, no chairs or pews. Everyone sat in physical and emotional intimacy on the floor, except my father. He sat beside me in his wheelchair, stroking my head, comforting me. Disregarding doctor's orders, he stayed for the entire ceremony.

The leaders of the mosque, the Mukhi and the Kamadia, offered prayers from the Qur'an. The Fathiha was recited. For two and a half hours, 1,400 souls joined in chanting the Salwat for the salvation of Tariq's soul while passing by his body in single file. The spiritual energy was electrifying.

Dan Pearson remembers:

"The closeness of the people sitting together on the floor intensified the sound and pulsation of the chanting. It became a mesmerizing balm. It had the impact of sweeping thoughts of sorrow from the mind, leaving peacefulness and a heightened sense of awareness. Everything seemed to be passing in slow motion—as if events were purposefully being recorded in our memories at a slower pace so they could later be remembered with clarity, and without pain. This wasn't about grief. This was about respect for the soul, awe for the soul.

"The heightened, painless sense of awareness from the chanting stayed with me a full 24 hours. Everyone who was there and tells of the event does so with reverence and without pain or grief, as though they had just witnessed a natural event: the passage of a soul. Even today, when I recall the events and the occasion, that sense of calmness returns. I am sure that is the intent of the chanting."

After everyone had filed by Tariq and paid their respects, the Mukhi nodded. It was time. Ten or 12 men placed the body in the funeral litter. Long wooden bars along each side of the litter extended to create two handles in front and two in back, much like a stretcher. Five hundred men formed two lines facing each other. The lines stretched 200 yards to the waiting hearse.

I took my position in front of the litter. The men who had placed Tariq's body on the litter raised it and rested the front handles on my shoulders, the back handles held by one of the mourners. I held one bar in each hand, looking down the two rows of men. Then I began my procession, walking slowly between the rows.

As I went by, the handles of the litter were passed from hand to hand. Each of the men of my faith community supported the litter in turn, helping me carry my burden. The litter rocked and swayed back and forth, like a boat riding gentle waves, as it made its way through the hands and the silence. Finally, the body was placed in the hearse.

I led the procession to the gravesite. My mind and emotions at this time were so full that it is difficult to make sense of them. Again, I'll call on Dan's recollection:

"Azim arrived at the gravesite and stepped from the car. He seemed stunned at the number of people present. The hundreds of men had reassembled, and stood silently under the gray afternoon sky.

"Following Ismaili ritual, he was invited to enter the grave and accept his son's body. He jumped in. The rain had rendered the earth wet and sodden; his feet sank into the mud. Tariq's body was handed to him. He held his son's head in his hands for the last time, and laid his body on the bier.

"He straightened, mud clinging to the knees of his suit, and looked up. His hand stretched up to me, out of the grave. I reached down to help him climb out. Our eyes met. His eyes had a look I had never seen before: it was as if he'd just had an extraordinary experience or reached a new depth of under-standing. And he hesitated—as if he were debating for a moment whether to stay in the grave with his son!

"Then he took my hand and came out of the grave, shaking and unsteady, to rejoin the world. I had a sudden feeling he had talked to Tariq one last time—and been told to continue with life until it was time for them to meet again. The look on his face was that of a man who had just finished a conversation. I think Tariq told him they must now take separate journeys, and gave him permission to return to the living.

"Azim placed the first shovel of dirt on the grave, then moved to a position a few feet away. I stood on one side of him, and his brother stood on the other. Each of the men walked by the grave in single file to place a shovel of dirt. Then they came to over to Azim to offer a brief prayer. Each person repeated the same prayer: an individual, chant-like ritual.

"The ritual ended. Azim returned to the grave and stood looking down. Watching him, I felt a chill. I had the feeling he was again fighting an inner call to join his son. I moved closer to him, stopping a few steps away. Alarmed, I tried to say something. I couldn't. Something took hold of my throat and my chest and said, 'Don't go there; don't speak.' I stood there, frozen. Then the chill faded. A slight smile crossed Azim's face, and he silently mouthed the words, 'I will.'"

The burial ceremony was over. Everyone had gone. I stood alone, looking at the grave. Dan's "chill" had been right on the mark—brother reading brother. For one moment, I *had* felt an overwhelming urge to jump in my son's grave and stay there.

I finally turned to leave. Dan was waiting for me. He helped me into the car, and we started back to the mosque, where the women of our family and faith community awaited us with a traditional lunch. According to Ismaili custom, women do not go to the gravesite for the burial ceremony. But as the car drove away, Dan noticed several of the women standing at the edge of the cemetery, still watching.

───────

More than once over the next few days, as the awful and painful truth of my son's murder continued to sink in, I considered leaving my adopted country. I remembered once telling Tariq and Tasreen that the best thing I had ever done for them was to make them United States citizens. How hollow those words now rang.

But thoughts of leaving quickly faded. I couldn't run away—from what had happened, or from the country I still loved. I started to feel anger: what was happening in our society that would turn killers loose on a college student delivering pizzas? But anger happens in any relationship, no matter how committed. The anger would have to be channeled. The energy it produced would have to be combined with my spiritual beliefs to address the problems that had unleashed the messenger of death. Tariq's death must be made meaningful.

No, I wasn't going anywhere.

───────

Three weeks after Tariq's death, however, I did have to go somewhere: Sofia, the capital of Bulgaria. I didn't want to go. I didn't feel anywhere near strong enough to return to business as usual. But a major deal was pending there, and I owed it to my clients to try to finish it. I spent five days in Sofia—the longest, hardest days of my life.

Before Tariq's death, I put unlimited energy into my work. Hundred-hour work weeks were commonplace. Now it took all my willpower just to get out of bed. My work as an international investment banker now had no meaning, no purpose. I was a financial strategist, paid to think. The last thing in the world I wanted to do now was think.

The late February winds of Sofia blew cold, grim, bitter, matching my mood. I struggled to keep my mind on business during the day; at night, I struggled to sleep. My doctor had given me sleeping pills. They didn't help.

In the evenings, unable to stay in the small hotel room, I'd leave the hotel and walk aimlessly for hours: no direction, no destination. Exhausted and chilled to the bone, I'd finally catch a taxi back to the hotel.

I had no one to talk to. The antiquated telephone system proved virtually useless for international calling. No one could reach me, and I couldn't reach my family. I felt terribly alone. Thoughts of suicide flashed through my mind. I found it impossible to picture myself ever smiling or laughing again.

During business meetings I feigned an interest which no longer existed. I drifted helplessly in a black hole, impenetrable to light. For years, I had meditated every morning. Now I couldn't, just as I couldn't eat or sleep.

The hellish trip finally ended. I returned home looking like a ghost.

––––––––––

In the Ismaili faith, special prayers are recited for the departed soul at the funeral; then 10 days, 40 days, 3 months, 6 months, a year, and every year after the death of a loved one. I returned to Vancouver from Bulgaria the day before the 40-day prayers.

During the prayers, one of my spiritual teachers offered a small flicker of light: something to move toward, which might give my life meaning. "After passing from this world," he said, "the soul remains in close proximity to the family and loved ones during the 40 days of grieving. After 40 days, the soul moves to a new level of consciousness. Grieving past this time impedes the soul's journey.

"It is human to grieve. But I recommend that you break the paralysis of grief, and find a good deed to do in Tariq's name. Compassionate acts undertaken in the name of the departed are spiritual currency, which will transfer to Tariq's soul and help speed his journey."

I didn't understand. Why would grief impede Tariq's journey?

"Life on earth is much more difficult than in the spiritual realm," my teacher said. "The departed soul is quite happy on the other side. Your son has completed his assignment here. You are not grieving for his discomfort. You are feeling sorry for yourself. Instead, do something good in his name. It will be good for you. It will be good for the recipient of your deed. It will be good for Tariq's soul."

Good deeds as spiritual currency. The wisdom and philosophy rang true for me. I glimpsed a path that would take me out of my morbid, paralyzed state. Perhaps this tragic incident could be made into an opportunity. Perhaps I could provide high-octane jet fuel for my son's bardo, and my own soul's progress towards enlightenment as well.

Tariq had completed his assignment here. Mine was just beginning.

Murder

. . . of all the bonds that can link societies, America epitomizes the strongest. It is called hope. The right to hope is the most powerful human motivation I know.

His Highness the Aga Khan,
Baccalaureate address at Brown University,
May 26, 1996

Criminal Justice

Murder is unique in that it abolishes the party it injures, so that society has to take the place of the victim and on his behalf demand atonement or grant forgiveness; it is the one crime in which society has a direct interest.

W.H. Auden, *The Guilty Vicarage*

Before I could chart my path forward, I had to know the truth: Who had killed Tariq? And why?

The mystery would unfold quickly.

The starting point was a small apartment above a carport in a dreary building on Alabama Street. The building appeared to be approaching its 40th birthday—and not aging gracefully. Unrepaired holes gaped in the stucco walls. A corroded iron gate led to the alley in back, where the decaying contents of an open dumpster filled both the air and unwary nasal passages. A copious population of flies celebrated the contents of the dumpster. Well-worn concrete provided the primary land-scaping motif.

The apartment was home to an 18-year-old girl, her younger sister, her younger brother, and the sister's 1-year-old daughter. Visitors were frequent. A variety of trouble-edged teens liked to hang out there enjoying music, recreational substances, video games, and momentary conjugal rites with each other.

It was also the informal command center and safe house for members of the gang called the Black Mob. They stored weapons and marijuana in the apartment.

The Black Mob was an inner city-style gang of sorts, but the members were not all products of poverty, and the environment around the Alabama Street apartment is not really inner city. Run-down, yes. Cheerless, to some eyes. Heading in the wrong direction, maybe. But it's a low-end, middle-class setting, not a slum. Carefully nurtured flowers grow in front of some of the mostly tiny houses. And the apartment buildings have received the basics of structural maintenance, even if esthetics have not been emphasized.

The Black Mob was not a high-profile organization. It had about 25 members, mostly midadolescents. Led by an 18-year-old named Antoine "Q-Tip" Pittman, they had specialized in the pettier variety of crimes. A month before Tariq's killing, though, Q-Tip had made the leap to the most heinous of crimes: murder. He shot and killed a drunken vagrant.

Q-Tip bragged about the killing. He said he had done it because he wanted to try out the gun. The act added substantially to the awe and intimidation he inspired in some of his young gang subordinates. Others got scared and left the gang.

On Friday night, January 20, the gang burglarized a house. One item of booty from the burglary was an addition to their weapons arsenal: a 9mm semiautomatic handgun.

Saturday night, January 21, several teenagers were hanging out at the Alabama Street apartment. Q-Tip was there. So were three 14-year-old boys: Solomon Simpson, whose nickname was "Solo"; Hakeem "Hook" Dunn; and a baby-faced kid called "Bone." His real name was Tony Hicks.

Tony Hicks' life did not get off to a great start.

His mother, Loeta, gave birth to Tony at age 15. His father, the same age, became a heavy drug user and veteran of the well-chronicled South Central Los Angeles gang scene. Tony had seen his father very few times during his life. The prominent feature of most of those meetings was the beating he was given by his sire.

Mike Reynolds, a San Diego writer and filmmaker, spent considerable time with Tony during his pretrial incarceration, and found a further indicator of Tony's early life environment: when he was nine, Tony had sex with his favorite uncle's girlfriend.

About that time, Loeta realized Tony had no chance of a decent life in her care on the streets of South Central. She asked Ples Felix, her father and Tony's grandfather, if Tony could live with him in San Diego.

Ples understood the issues well. He had grown up in the South Central environment himself, fathering Loeta when he was only 16. Unlike most, Ples had made it out of the mean streets to a successful life. He joined the merchant marine, then the Army. He became a Green Beret, serving two tours in Vietnam. He eventually went to college, earned a graduate degree, and now holds a responsible job for the City of San Diego.

Ples felt up to the task of raising his grandchild, of introducing Tony to the right values and healthy discipline. Perhaps it represented a chance to atone for his absence from Loeta's early life. Tony and Ples developed a warm, loving relationship.

By age 14, though, adolescents are developing their own sense of priorities. Fun, rebellion and peers often outrank discipline, values and parents. Tony began to chafe against Ples' strict rules for living in his house. He preferred hanging out

Above: Tony at age 9 with his mother, Loeta, and grandfather, Ples.

Left: Tony at 14, dressed for church.

with the gang. The gang was putting pressure on him to do it more, partly to replace the membership loss following the killing of the vagrant. Tony started doing it more.

Tony kept his gang activities hidden. Ples had no idea what was going on until he came home on Saturday, January 21, and found a note from his grandson: *Daddy, I love you. But I've run away. Tony.*

The note deeply worried Ples. He became even more worried when he discovered that Tony had taken more than just his video games, a package of corn nuts, and some change off the dresser. Ples' shotgun was gone also.

————————

The quotes which follow are from Mike Reynolds' transcript (somewhat paraphrased) of his interviews with Tony:

I was mad at Daddy. We got into a fight on Friday night about a pink slip I got for skippin' school on Thursday. Hakeem and I spent the day kickin' it and smokin' bud [marijuana]. Daddy didn't know about the bud but was trippin' on the pink slip. It was Saturday, he was gone when I got up, but he left me a bunch of chores to do. I didn't care about the usual stuff, but this list was crazy, gonna keep me goin' all day and I had plans.

Daddy and me were arguing a lot. He was strict. I had to be in every night by dark, but none of my friends had to come home until curfew kicked in at 10:00. My homeboys were startin' to tease me about it. Daddy wanted me to be the perfect little boy. I didn't want to be perfect and I wasn't little no more.

*I left the note where Daddy would find it. I went to
Hakeem's. Then we got Solomon and went to another
dude's to smoke some bud. Then we went to Alabama
Street to see what was goin' on.*

*I told them I was goin' to L.A. and I needed money.
I knew where Daddy kept a gauge [shotgun] so we went
back to the house to get it; thought I could sell it and get
enough to get me to L.A.*

*I gave Solo my key and he went in. Hook and I
kept a lookout. I knew I was in deep now; there was no
way Daddy was gonna forget about this.*

*Solo broke a window to make it look like a
burglary. Solo was always thinkin'. He stuffed the gauge
down his pants and we started back to Alabama. Solo
went down the alley limpin' like a fool. Hakeem said if
we saw any cops we'd have to shoot them.*

*Q-Tip thought the gauge was cool and wanted to
keep it. They stuck it in Pa-Ru's closet. [Pa-Ru was a
nickname for Paul, the younger brother of the girl who
rented the apartment.] I was thinkin', "What about my
money?"*

*We smoked some more weed. 'Cause they took my
damn gauge, we had to go back to my house to get
some money. I wanted my Sega, too. I was thinkin',
"Man, Daddy's gonna kill me already so I might as well
really get him mad."*

*Went back to Alabama and kicked it for the rest of
the day. Homies came and went. We smoked bud,
played vids and I think some of them were drinkin' 40s
[40-ounce bottles] of malt liquor.*

*Nothin' happened the rest of the day until later
when I got hungry.*

———————

Around 8:30 PM, the group at the Alabama Street apartment got hungry for pizza. Lack of money was no deterrent. Tony suggested a solution they were familiar with: the "jacking" of a pizza delivery man.

Q-Tip planned the "jack." They would select a phony address and call in an order to be delivered there. When the delivery man showed up, he and Bone would hassle and distract the pizza man. Solo and Hook would snatch the pizzas. Easy.

Tony and Hook left the apartment to check out potential sites for the "jack." Two blocks away, they found a modest-sized apartment house on Louisiana Street. The apartments had individual addresses. They decided they would confuse the delivery man by specifying apartment "D" in this building.

*The pizza man would find the right building, but
he wasn't gonna find no place to deliver it 'cause there
wasn't no apartment D.*

Tony and Hook returned to the Alabama Street apartment with the results of their recon mission. Two girls were also there that night. The boys asked one of them, a 16-year-old aspiring rap star with a mature voice, to call in the order. She did—to San Diego Giant Pizza. If they had taken the order, Tariq would be alive today. But by this time it was 9:30, past their delivery time. So she called their second choice: DiMille's Italian

Restaurant. She ordered two large pizzas, giving a fake name and telephone number, and the Louisiana Street address.

For her part in the "jack," the girl was promised two slices of pizza.

The pizzas came out of the oven, and were given to Tariq to deliver. The Black Mob headed out for the two-block walk to the setup site on Louisiana Street. Despite the reservations of one of the boys, they brought the gang's newly acquired 9mm handgun. Q-Tip decided Tony should carry it.

Q-Tip told Solo to give me the strap. He didn't think I would do nothin' with it. Solo had a bad temper and Hook was crazy so Q-Tip figured I was the best one to hold it. He didn't know how mad I was at everyone and everything.

Q-Tip wasn't gonna hold it 'cause he was 18 and could get in a lot more trouble than us kids if we got caught.

When Tariq arrived at the apartment complex, he saw immediately that there was no match with the apartment number he'd been given. He paid no attention to the four boys leaning against a brick wall across the street. To their great amusement, he entered the apartment complex with his pizzas and started knocking on doors, trying to find out who had placed the order.

Pizza man went into the apartment building. We heard him poundin' on doors, askin' people if they ordered a pizza. It was pretty funny. He came back to the street and he was trippin'. Pizza man was real mad by now.

Tariq emerged from the apartment building. He put the pizzas back into the car and slammed the hatch. He turned around. Tony and Q-Tip were facing him.

I took out the nine and crossed the street. Q-Tip was behind me. When pizza man turns around, he's starin' at me and the nine. I said, "Give me the pizzas." Pizza man just looks at me, goes to get in the car like he don't care I'm pointin' a gun at him.

Tariq and Jennifer had discussed what he would do if he were ever confronted with an attempted robbery. Jennifer had told him not to be a hero, but Tariq was principled and feisty. Despite his diminutive stature, he was not afraid of anyone. He issued an angry retort to the demand to surrender his cargo, and climbed into his Volkswagen.

He gets in the car. I'm really mad now. What's this world comin' to? He starts the car, rolls up the window, and starts to back up. I go 'long side the car, pointin' the gun at him, not knowin' what to do. I pull the slide back and jack a bullet into the nine.

Tariq was backing out of the driveway. In 20 seconds he'd be driving down the street away from this madness. He probably didn't believe anyone would shoot him, or anybody, for two pizzas. Maybe he thought they were bluffing and he wasn't really in danger. Maybe his stubborn sense of right and wrong kicked in, and he was willing to risk danger.

Q-Tip starts shoutin' at me, "Bust him, Bone, bust
him!" So I did. I pulled the trigger. The nine kicks hard,
the window broke, and pizza man yelled. Blood was
comin' out of him. I knew he was hurt bad.

The last words Tariq uttered in this life were, "Help me!
No! No!" The shot, through a rolled-up window, into a moving
car, from the hand of an inexperienced gunman, could have gone
anywhere. It could have missed completely. It could have in-
flicted an insignificant wound. But it didn't. It penetrated Tariq's
shoulder, and continued through his left lung, then his heart,
then his right lung. The car shuddered to a stop. The Black Mob
ran down the street and disappeared. They were seen by a man
walking his dog, who would later report what he saw to the
investigating police.

In the Volkswagen, the pizzas and my son's body grew cold
in the January night air. In his pocket, the delivery slip showed
the amount due for the order: $27.24.

———————

Later, Mike Reynolds reported, Tony said a lot of strange
things happened during the few moments he spent on earth
with Tariq. He said a light was shining down from heaven, on
just the two of them, as if they were the only people in the world.

———————

The gang returned to the Alabama Street apartment, and
turned on the television. Sure enough, within a few minutes,
news of the shooting was being broadcast to San Diego residents.

The gang felt comfortable they had left no clues to connect them to the crime.

It was all cool. I didn't think I was gonna get in trouble. Only homeboys saw what happened and they weren't gonna snitch. The guy with the dog didn't see nothin'.

But not everyone involved was a homeboy. On Monday, the San Diego Police Department's Homicide Team Two got a big break. The girl who had phoned in the pizza order called and left a message on the Child Safety Network Trust (CSN) hotline. As Ward Leber had hoped might happen, she had seen the number on television. She was frightened. She wanted to remain anonymous. She was afraid of Q-Tip. But she was also afraid that she would be condemned to hell for her part in the murder. She wanted to talk.

"I know what happened," said the message she left on the CSN answering machine. "I know who did this." She left a telephone number where she could be reached.

Melody Argentine worked at the CSN office in Huntington Beach, California. When she got home from work Monday night, on a hunch, she called her office to check the machine for messages. Her hunch was right. She immediately called the girl back. She got the girl to agree to meet with police detectives in the morning.

On Tuesday morning, the girl changed her mind. She was petrified of Q-Tip. She was sure he'd come after her if she snitched. The meeting was off, then on again, then off again as the girl struggled with the confusing mixture of pressure and conflict. Finally, Melody convinced her to go ahead with the meeting.

She met with Homicide Team Two. She downplayed her own role, telling them she was not aware there was going to be a robbery. And she told them the names of the four boys responsible for the death of my son.

The police had no trouble finding Tony. He was already in custody. Ples had sadly done what he knew he must when he discovered his shotgun missing. He called the police, reported it stolen, and told them that the thief was probably his grandson. They arrested Tony for the shotgun theft before they knew of his involvement in the slaying.

> *They ask me about the shotgun and I tell them I sold it. I'm thinkin' maybe they're gonna bust me for the shotgun, maybe they don't know nothin' about me and pizza man.*

On Wednesday, Pittman and the other two boys were arrested and brought in for questioning. With the information they had gotten from the girl, and their own investigation, they had enough facts to convince the boys they were in trouble.

> *I knew somethin' bad was up when we get to headquarters and the cops turn me over to some homicide detectives. They told me everything they knew and that was plenty to bust my ass good. I wasn't gonna snitch no one out so I told them I did it. I told them I*

*killed the pizza man. They asked me who was with me
and I made some stuff up, I wasn't gonna help no cops. I
did tell them that pizza man was stupid; he should have
give up the pizzas.*

Of all the wrenching effects to flow from my son's death,
Tony's path from that last sentence to his eventual courtroom
statement was to be one of the most remarkable.

––––––––––

Mike Reynolds wrote:

"Tony said he had time before shooting to think about his
options. He could throw the gun away and let the pizza man
go, but that would have angered Q-Tip and the others. He could
shoot Q-Tip but he wasn't sure how Solo and Hook would react
to that. He could shoot himself. Or he could shoot the pizza
man.

"The pizza man meant nothing to him. In Tony's world,
shooting Tariq made the most sense.

"Tony said he knew he would never make it to 30 without
being sent to prison or killed. He was wrong. He didn't make it
to 15."

––––––––––

A unique legal drama soon began to unfold, interleaving
its impact with the story of the killing itself. On Tuesday, April
4, 1995, *The San Diego Union-Tribune* newspaper printed a
startling headline: "DA wants boys tried as adults." The story
went on to say,

Making his first appearance in court since he was elected district attorney, Paul Pfingst urged a Superior Court judge yesterday to try two juveniles accused in the robbery and shooting death of a pizza delivery man as adults.

The defendants could become the first 14-year-olds in California to be tried as adults under a state law enacted this year . . .

"There'll be resistance to the idea of trying them as adults, but I'm here to change it, and we're on very sound ground.

"I want 14- and 15-year-olds in the county to know they run the risk of being tried as adults," he said. "Most of them think they're immune."

The decision to try the 14-year-olds as adults under California's new law, passed just three weeks before Tariq's killing, generated enormous controversy. Discussions were energetic. Opinions quickly became polarized.

Arguments in favor of adult trials were based on strong human emotion. The need for law and order. Deterrence of violent crime. Justice. Punishment. Revenge. Many people saw Tariq's slaying as an exercise in simple, old-fashioned greed and cruelty, regardless of the age of the offenders.

Like other states, California has been in a desperate battle to curb criminal activity. People want to feel safe again. In addition to the new law permitting criminals as young as 14 to be tried as adults for murder, California recently passed a "three strikes" law mandating tough sentences for repeat offenders.

There has also been fear and anger everywhere about the increasingly violent acts being committed by children, and by teenagers who are really still children. In San Diego County alone, recent crimes have included a 17-year-old boy killing his parents, grandparents, and young sister. An 11-year-old boy put on a monk's robe, shaved his head, and went on a shooting spree. Three teenagers—ages 15, 16 and 18—stabbed a 53-year-old woman to death.

In northern California, a 6-year-old boy beat an infant nearly to death. Also in northern California, four boys age 12 to 14 were arrested and charged with the rape of a 10-year-old girl.

In Chicago, two 10-year-olds threw a 4-year-old out a window to his death.

In Kentucky, a 14-year-old boy shot into a high school prayer circle, killing 3 and wounding 5.

In Arkansas, a 13-year-old and an 11-year-old opened fire on schoolmates, killing 4 girls and a teacher, and wounding 11 others.

The list goes on and on.

In the next seven years, there will be 500,000 more teenagers in the U.S. than today. If current trends are allowed to persist, 6 percent, or 30,000 of them, will become felons.

We have a serious problem on our hands.

The argument against adult trials for these boys was based on the concept that no matter how heinous the crime, a 14-year-old can't be considered mature enough to have truly understood the act of murder and its consequences. Fourteen-year-olds cannot act from adult will and conviction. They are merely the product of circumstance at this age, not yet in charge of their own destiny. Most of all, they are too young to throw away. They must be given the chance for rehabilitation and restoration.

In Tony Hicks' case, other arguments were put forth: he was high on marijuana at the time of the shooting; he was under duress from having just run away from the home of a controlling grandfather; he felt abandoned by his mother; he was fearful of Q-Tip.

The stakes for the boys were huge. In the juvenile justice system, regardless of the crime for which they were convicted, their maximum penalty would be confinement to a California Youth Authority facility until age 25. Then they would be unconditionally released—no probation or parole requirements—and given the chance to start building a new life.

If convicted of first-degree murder, trial as an adult could bring a sentence of life in prison.

While the criminal justice system wrangling took place, the issues were swirling around my attempts to grapple with the loss of Tariq. I hadn't thought it out yet. I couldn't, until I got further along in dealing with my grief. But the "eye for an eye" approach didn't seem like the answer. Nothing could bring Tariq back. But if these boys could somehow be saved, shouldn't they be? Weren't they victims, too? I still could not find it in my heart to crave vengeance.

The defense attorneys for the boys filed a constitutional challenge. They lost. The new law's constitutionality was upheld.

Eventually, it was decided that Solomon "Solo" Simpson and Hakeem "Hook" Dunn would be tried as juveniles. But Tony Hicks had pulled the trigger; he would not be granted juvenile status. The court's ruling meant that he would become the youngest Californian in the history of the state to be tried as an adult. The charge: murder in the first degree.

Also coming up on the court's agenda was the trial of 18-year-old Antoine "Q-Tip" Pittman.

———

A vital part of my Ismaili belief is the sanctity of the soul of each and every human being, and the journey of that soul. Never has that belief been so challenged as it has been with Antoine "Q-Tip" Pittman. Never have I come so close to feeling that here might be a human without a soul.

On December 4, 1995, Pittman's trial opened. He was charged with second-degree murder in the killing of a drunk transient named Lonnie Smithwick, and first-degree murder in the slaying of my son.

He was not charged with leading young boys down the road to hell. But of that grave crime he was certainly guilty.

Lonnie Smithwick had been killed on the night of December 23, 1994. Pittman was in the company of a juvenile named Aniece "Wicked" Jamaal. Smithwick was drunk, harmless, just hanging around a liquor store with his hands in his pockets. Pittman and "Wicked" had gone to the store around 11 PM to buy some chips. As they left the store, Pittman confronted Smithwick and they exchanged a few words. "Wicked" was totally freaked out when Pittman pulled the gun and fired, and Smithwick collapsed, his hands still in his pockets. He died instantly, the victim of senseless, profitless cruelty.

A series of witnesses pieced together an incontrovertible story of Pittman's involvement in Tariq's death. His attorney's strategy was probably the only thing it could have been: an attempt to portray the key witnesses as liars on a self-serving mission. The preponderance of evidence doomed this strategy to failure.

Despite the publicity, few people were in the courtroom during the trial. I was not there. My emotional state made it impossible for me to attend.

On December 27, 1995, the jury found Antoine "Q-Tip" Pittman guilty on both counts of murder. His sentence: life in prison without the possibility of parole. His visible reaction to his sentence: absolutely none.

———

Solomon Simpson and Hakeem Dunn pled guilty to second-degree murder in juvenile court. They will spend the next several years in youth detention facilities, and will be released in their early twenties.

That left Tony.

When the judge ruled that Tony would be tried as an adult despite the impassioned pleas of his attorneys, Tony began crying in the courtroom. The defense team had argued that he could be completely rehabilitated through a maximum sentence to the California Youth Authority.

"He's only 14," public defender Jeff Reilly told the judge. "We could practically undo every day that he's been alive in 10½ years."

Attorney William La Fond used language that *The San Diego Union-Tribune* called "poetic":

"He is anxious, he is unhappy with who he is, and that is precisely the engine that will drive him to change. . . . We have seen how easy it is to damage a child and corrupt his spirit. We can convince him that he is unlovable and that he is responsible for his pathetic life. Lost in this fog of despair, this child is wounded and he is dying. . . . You [Judge Federico Castro] have a godlike power to determine whether these souls go down the road to salvation or to damnation."

However, Prosecutor Peter Deddeh argued that Tony had already been given the opportunity to turn his life around. His grandfather was providing love, direction, stability—all the necessary ingredients—and probably doing it better than the California Youth Authority could. "Yet, with all the love, all the structure, all the discipline," Deddeh said, ". . . he still ends up a gang member and a murderer."

Deddeh also pointed out that the only remorse Tony had shown was a letter to a friend lamenting the fact that he couldn't score any marijuana in jail.

While others talked and external events progressed, something was going on inside Tony.

Perhaps it was the effect of the frequent visits and loving support from Ples Felix.

Perhaps it was a response to hearing from Ples and Mike Reynolds that I considered him a victim also; that I was not keeping the flame of hate burning; that I did not seek vengeance. What I wanted at that point—and Mike had told him this—was for him to face a jury and tell the story. I wanted him to ask our family to forgive him. I wanted him to ask for God's forgiveness for taking another person's life. I had not yet heard of the concept called "restorative justice," which now means so much to me. But somehow I felt if he did these things, he—and I— could start on a path to healing.

Perhaps what he heard about the work we had started through the Tariq Khamisa Foundation (discussed in detail in the chapter entitled, "You *Do* Have A Choice") touched his heart.

Maybe it was just that many days alone in his cell gave him the time and the environment to consider what he had done in a different light.

I like to think his soul was waking and growing.

Mike Reynolds said that during one of their discussions, Tony wanted to know if Jesus was reincarnated when He rose from the dead.

On April 11, 1996, after more than a year of legal procedure, maneuvering, wrangling, words, papers and hearings, Tony entered the courtroom and faced San Diego Superior Court Judge Joan Weber.

"I understand you want to change your plea, Mr. Hicks," the judge said. Tony confirmed that he did. He then pled guilty to premeditated murder of my son: murder in the first degree.

Henry Coker, Tony's attorney at that stage, said that Tony was emotionally devastated by his crime, and exhausted by the legal process. He did not want to subject his family, my family or himself to the ordeal that a trial, with its replay of the fatal evening's events, would have brought.

"He's extremely remorseful about what happened," Coker was quoted as saying. "He just doesn't want to cause any more pain . . . He now realizes he made a mistake, and some mistakes you just can't fix."

Sentencing was set for June 18.

———

"I have been dreading this day," Judge Weber said on June 18. "There is no pleasure in sentencing a boy to prison." Then she echoed the same view which had been haunting me for over a year: "I essentially see two lives destroyed by this."

Many people spoke at the sentencing. None was more eloquent than Tony himself. Here is the statement he wrote with the help of one of his defense attorney's staff members, and read aloud in the courtroom:

Good morning, Judge.

On January 21, 1995, I shot and killed Tariq Khamisa; a person I didn't even know and who didn't do anything wrong to me. On April 11, 1996, I pled guilty to first-degree murder because I am guilty. I wanted to save the Khamisa family and my family from further pain.

From my grandfather, I have learned about the Khamisa family and their only son Tariq. I have learned about the love they have for him. Through my grandfather and Mr. Reynolds, they have tried to explain to me the compassion the Khamisa family has for me.

I have had a lot of problems in my life. Over the last year, while I have been in Juvenile Hall, I have thought about my problems. I wish I didn't have the type of life I had. I wish I had a relationship with my father. I think about the warmth that my grandfather gave me. I wonder why I didn't listen and learn. Now, I wish I would have listened to my grandfather.

At night, when I'm alone, I cry and beg God to let me out of here. I promise Him that I will be a better person—I won't mess up. When I see my mom, I want to hold her as tight as I can, and beg her, 'Take me out of jail!'

However, I don't want to use my problems as an excuse for my actions. I think I would have gone to jail sometime but I honestly don't think getting busted for a robbery or something like that would have changed me. I was too mad at everyone: my mom, my dad, my grandfather. When I first came to the Hall I was mad at the D.A. and the people at the Hall for keeping me here. Now, I'm just scared and mad at myself.

I'm alone at Juvenile Hall. Even though the people at the Hall are pretty cool, I'm still alone. I often think about the night I shot Tariq, especially when I'm alone in my cell. When it's dark and quiet, I wonder what it's like to die. I wonder why I'm still alive. Sometimes when I roll over in bed and I lay next to the cold wall, I feel as far away from everything as possible. I wonder if that's what dying feels like.

I still don't know why I shot Tariq. I didn't really want to hurt him or anyone else. I'm sorry. I'm sorry for killing Tariq and hurting his family. I'm sorry for the pain that I caused for Tariq's father, Mr. Khamisa. I pray to God every day that Mr. Khamisa will forgive me for what I have done, and for as long as I live I will continue to pray to God to give him strength to deal with his loss.

My grandfather promised me that he will be Mr. Khamisa's friend and help him in any way he can for the rest of his life. I am very sorry for what I have done. Thank you for giving me the chance to speak.

I have reflected, often and deeply, on the distance between this statement and *I did tell them that pizza man was stupid; he should have give up the pizzas.*

———————

Mike Reynolds looked back on his conversations with Tony:

"Even with the love and support Tony got from Ples, there was the other side of Tony—the side that didn't buy any of Ples' love and discipline—the side that didn't want to buy it.

"But during our meetings, we told him about the Tariq Khamisa Foundation, and about the work it was going to do. Tony was a great listener. When his change actually occurred, I don't know. But we kept giving him the same message. I think Tony wouldn't believe for a long time that the father of the son he killed actually felt anything for him, other than the need to rip him apart.

"But gradually, we brought him into a way of thinking that is so foreign to these kids. We kept him posted on what was going on at the Foundation, and he was very involved. Eventually, he gained awareness of the consequences of what he had done, and his responsibility for it. And he must have started to realize that Azim's feelings of compassion for him were real.

"It must have been an amazing thing for the kid who committed the act to find himself involved with the other side—something I'm sure he never envisioned.

"When I first met the kid I didn't want to like him. This kid had killed someone for absolutely nothing. I've been in the military, and around death and guns and shooting and dying. I had no sympathy for him. I thought, 'Tony Hicks deserves everything he's gonna get.'

"But maybe Azim had a premonition. From very early on, he said he didn't hold anything against this kid. And I didn't believe it! I'm more of an 'eye for an eye' guy. But the more time I spent with Tony, and the more time I spent with Azim, the more I realized that Azim was right: this kid was also, in some respects, a victim. He pulled the trigger, yes. He killed Azim's son, yes. But inside Tony, there *is* a nice kid, a kid who didn't want to kill another person. But he was immature, emotional, angry, stoned; a lot had happened to him in the 24 hours before the shooting—and Tariq ended up in the wrong place at the wrong time. "

———

Judge Weber pronounced sentence on Tony: 25 years to life in prison. He will be eligible for parole when he is 37 years old.

Tony's mother, Loeta, was at the sentencing. They gave each other a brief farewell embrace. Tears filled their eyes. Then Tony was led away by a uniformed officer.

Tony will be in a juvenile facility until he is 18. Then he will probably be transferred to state prison. There he will pass from what is left of his adolescence, to begin what will be his adulthood.

He killed my son. Still, I will pray that his life may yet bring value and goodness to others and to himself.

———

The criminal justice system had spoken. It had done what it does. But it was too late, and it was not enough. No one was healed. I knew I had to pledge myself to finding a way for all of us to do more, to do better, in the struggle to overcome the tragedy of youth violence.

Criminal Justice

Be a lamp, or a lifeboat, or a ladder
Help someone's soul heal
Walk out of your house like a shepherd

Jelaluddin Rumi, 13th century Persian Sufi poet,
The Diwan of Shams of Tabriz, no. 3090

My Ismaili Path

*A route differs from a road . . . because (a route) is
merely a line that connects one point with another. A
route has no meaning in itself; its meaning derives
entirely from the two points that it connects. A road is a
tribute to space. Every stretch of road has meaning in
itself and invites us to stop.*

Milan Kundera, *Immortality*

hy?

That's the question people ask about my reaction to Tariq's
death. Why didn't I want an eye for an eye? Why, even through
crushing grief, did the desire for vengeance not take hold? I've
heard that "why?" many times. It has driven me to long, hard
bouts of probing introspection in search of an answer. And the
straight answer is: I'm still not sure. But my response was
immediate, and true to whatever is in my soul.

When I find that answer, I'm sure its roots will spring from
my Ismaili path.

If a movie were made about the migrations of our family
and ancestors, it might be called *Out of Persia, Out of India, Out
of Africa, Out of Canada, Into America*. It has been a long and
winding road.

Azim's parents, Noordin and Remy

The spiritual leader of my Ismaili faith is known as the Imam. "Imam" means "Guide." An essential role of the Imam is to guide his followers on their trek for enlightenment. In the 1830s, the Shah of Persia granted the honorary, hereditary title of "Aga Khan" to the Ismaili Imam. The first Aga Khan had a falling out with the Shah in 1843. He left Persia for India, which already had a large Ismaili community. Many Persian Ismailis followed him. My ancestors were among them.

The third Aga Khan initiated a program to develop facilities, schools, institutions and businesses to serve the Ismaili community. The focus of these programs was mainly in the Indian subcontinent and in East Africa. During this period, many Ismailis left India for East Africa, settling largely in Zanzibar, Tanzania, Kenya and Uganda. My paternal grandfather arrived in Kenya from India in 1906.

My mother's family settled in Uganda, in the little town of Mbale. She would have been born there if my grandmother hadn't decided to take a trip back to India while very pregnant. My mother was born "on the road," in Bombay, India.

My father was born in the Kenyan town of Kisumu. In 1949, with the blood of Persia and India in my veins, so was I.

Our family business provided a comfortable life. My father started an auto repair shop called "Rainbow Garage." Eventually, he also became a Peugeot dealer. The success of the business made it possible for my education to include schooling abroad. At 15, I went to England to continue my studies there.

I aced the accounting courses, finishing near the top and passing a test that only 18 percent of 18,000 students passed. If things had gone smoothly and according to plan, today I would probably be an African entrepreneur or a Kenyan CPA.

However, while I was in London my father had his first bout of heart trouble. As the oldest son, my responsibilities to family and community were clear. Although I would have loved to finish my education in London, I returned to Kenya at age 21 to work in the family business and prepare to run it.

My father recovered from his illness, and our company thrived. I expanded the scope of the business to include automobile-related financial services: leasing, lending and insurance. The financial expertise I gained during this period was to prove invaluable when circumstances forced us to liquidate everything and leave Kenya.

———————

A philosophical lesson I received from Dr. Harvey, one of my accounting instructors at South West London College, may have been worth more to me than everything he taught me about debits and credits. Despite our business successes, I had big concerns about the competitive outlook. The Japanese were making a substantial investment in developing an African market for their cars. They were moving into our area with large, well-financed dealerships. I returned to see Dr. Harvey 18 months after leaving to take over the family business and he asked me how I was doing.

"I'm doing well," I said. "We're still number one. But the Japanese are kicking us out. The Datsuns and the Toyotas and the Mazdas are showing up. I don't know if we can keep our dealership going and on top in this market."

"I'm very disappointed in you," he replied. "You were my star student. And now look at you. I'm very disappointed."

I was baffled and hurt. This man was like a god to me. I said, "Dr. Harvey, I added new subsidiaries to our business, and

I doubled our profits. I don't understand. I would have thought you'd be proud of me. Why are you so disappointed?"

"The reason I'm disappointed," he said, "is because you're looking over your shoulder, trying to see who is catching up from behind you. What I want to know is: what are you doing to catch up with the guy *ahead* of you?"

As his statement sunk in, I realized he had held up a mirror. In it, I saw the perspective I had fallen into. I was in a small town in Kenya. I had come to feel it was my kingdom—at least as far as the auto business was concerned. I was the top guy. And I was scared to death about not staying the top guy in this little corner. But there was a whole world out there.

To catch up with those ahead of me, I had to expand beyond my current, comfortable frontier. Dr. Harvey's words rang in my mind as I began changing our business to make it a national enterprise. We went into the big city, Nairobi. Sure enough: there was always somebody ahead of me, somebody I needed to catch and pass.

Now I'm doing business in America, the most dynamic economic environment of all. And I'm still grateful Dr. Harvey told me not to look over my shoulder. Success here requires the focus to be on the road ahead, not the route behind.

Before I went off to school in London in 1965, we threw a big party to celebrate my new adventure. At the party I met a girl named Almas. I spent the whole night flirting and dancing with her. I found out she had also been born in Kisumu, and lived there with her grandparents. Her parents lived in Fort Portal, Uganda—a beautiful area near the Mountain of the Moons.

Over the next few years, each time I came home from London for a visit, Almas and I dated. In 1971, once I returned to stay, we were married. Our daughter Tasreen was born in 1972.

————————

Africa is a continent of unpredictable forces—natural and political. In 1971, across the border from Kenya, a madman named Idi Amin came into power in the neighboring country of Uganda. He initiated a reign of terror and predation, devastating Uganda's agricultural sector. His purges ultimately took the lives of 300,000 Ugandans.

In an act that struck fear directly into our hearts, he began to expel people of Asian descent from the country. Almas' entire family was in that group. Amin's message of hatred and threats of violence toward our ethnic group (and others) could not be ignored. National borders offer limited protection in Africa, and tides of racism, once underway, can rise rapidly anywhere. We felt vulnerable and exposed. We decided we could not risk staying in such close proximity to the madness. We developed a plan by which the entire family would leave East Africa over the next two years.

At this critical hour for East African Ismailis, the country of Canada stepped in to provide a "safe harbor." Ismailis could go to the Canadian High Commission in the Ugandan capital of Kampala, and receive papers and an airplane ticket for emigration to Canada. The Canadian government even gave them heavy coats upon their arrival in Montreal.

The government also provided housing for those who had nowhere to go. But the Ismailis are a resourceful people with practical skills, a strong work ethic, and a deep commitment to community service. Many speak English in addition to their native language. Almost everyone quickly found their way into mainstream Canadian life.

Ismailis will never forget the graciousness Canada offered during this time of need. The welcome and support we received can never really be repaid. But on the first anniversary of the exodus, the Ismaili community gave a generous donation to Canada's United Way as a token of our appreciation.

———

I got my first investment banking experience in Kenya, on a project that would not have been my first choice for a maiden voyage: liquidating the family business. This was investment banking baptism by fire. Everyone was leaving and trying to sell something first. This made for a great buyer's market, but an abominable seller's market, and I was a seller.

One of my automobile customers ran a bank that had been established, with government help, to assist budding African entrepreneurs. I approached this man and showed him that our business was strong and viable, and worth continuing in local hands. Through him, I brought a group of four people together. They were responsible African businessmen, but very short on cash. I helped them create a bank loan application package. The proceeds would be used to buy our family business.

Kenya is a long way from America, but bankers are bankers wherever they are. The bankers sent an endless stream of engineers, loan officers, MBAs and paperwork to check us out. They knew we were in crisis mode, so they hurried the deal along. That meant it only took them one year and two months to agree to finance the purchase.

However, they wouldn't finance the whole thing. I had to do gravity-defying financial somersaults to find the rest. It was a glorious day when it finally came together.

I took a deep breath.

It had been a tough transaction, and it required one last commitment: my father had to agree to stay in Kenya for two years, to teach the buyers how to run their newly acquired business.

Completing the sale was only half the battle. An equally challenging part was getting the money out of the country, and being able to take it with us to start our new life in North America. Kenya is not a country with sophisticated financial systems. There was virtually no well-defined, official procedure for expatriating significant sums of money. So a tortuous, almost black-market-style transaction had to be used.

My dad and I knew an exporter we could work with. We paid him 25-30 percent over the market price for merchandise, and we structured a *very* complicated arrangement by which we could receive the proceeds outside the country when the merchandise was sold. This probably wasn't legal at the time, but everyone who needed to escape from East Africa was doing it, or trying to. My dad ended up helping many desperate people get their money out of the country through transactions similar to ours.

When the adventure was done, I looked back and realized that managing the sale of our business under complex and daunting circumstances had been an exhilarating challenge. I knew I would want more of that challenge.

An investment banker was born.

In some respects, our timing in leaving Kenya in 1973 was fortunate. Until 1979, when an invasion by Tanzanian troops and Ugandan exiles drove Amin's forces out and Amin into exile, that part of the world was turbulent and dangerous. But in one respect, our timing made things more difficult on ourselves: Almas was pregnant with Tariq during the move. He was born in Vancouver on March 6, 1974.

———

I came to Canada with $30,000—my share of the sale of the family business. My intent was to buy a business I could run. Dad was willing to be my partner and co-investor if I found the right opportunity. In the meantime, I hoped to find transactions I could broker or participate in as a paid adviser.

I sailed into my search with an optimism which soon became subdued. My success at selling our business in Kenya had probably given me too much confidence. I tried to put several deals together. Nothing happened the way I hoped it would. I was humbled.

The uncertainty of my family's living situation added pressure. I didn't want to settle into a permanent residence until we knew where our business would be and what we could afford. Almas and the children were living with her mother in Vancouver. The limited space in the house made everyone feel crowded and tense. She and I decided she should go back to Kenya, where my parents had a bigger house, and live with them until I could get things resolved.

She was there for seven months. During that period I saw her and the children only twice. I missed some of the precious early days in my infant son's development. This was not the good life.

After some false starts, I found a business situation I thought was a sure winner. The owners who were selling the business had serious problems with each other. They couldn't agree on the weather outside the window. With pit-bull perseverance, we worked through the obstacles. Then the lawyers entered the picture, and almost destroyed the deal.

The fact that we managed to consummate the transaction at all is probably a monument to the human spirit. But we did, and I was the proud part-owner of an American business: Sterling Food Company, a manufacturer of specialty bread mixes for grocery store bakeries.

By the end of 1974, I had obtained a green card allowing me to work in the United States, and rented a house in Seattle to be near my new business. I felt stabilized. I looked forward to bringing the family back together without the fear that I would have to keep moving them around like a band of traveling minstrels. Almas returned from Kenya and joined me in Seattle.

That rented house became the first American home we owned—and the first Ismaili mosque in Seattle. We bought it from a man named Alvin Brown, a person of great integrity and generosity, whom I met as a business associate. He became a friend, then a virtual family member, living with us for a few months. He was like a second father to me; the children called him Granddad. He was the first important American in my new life.

With the family settled, I threw myself into making a living for us. I quickly fell in love with the American entrepreneurial spirit. For a while it loved me, too. Then it sent me the business equivalent of a "Dear John" letter.

Between 1975 and 1980, I successfully invested in businesses and projects in Seattle, Dallas, Atlanta, and San Diego. I was flying high. I couldn't miss. My original $30,000 grew to $1.8 million. So this was America!

But everything in life is a package. As the workload and business demands increased, so did my stress level. My lifestyle started to deteriorate, and I was hardly aware of it. I smoked heavily. I stopped exercising. I didn't spend enough time with my family.

I found out this is not an uncommon story in the U.S. Perhaps I became Americanized a little too fast. Business success is so seductive; it's easy to let it override everything. We get away from the basics. We forget what's really important.

Success can go away. And we may find to our horror that everything else we need went away, too, because we neglected it. We can be left with nothing.

———————

Toward the end of the decade, my little business empire started to fall apart. We had financed part of our activities with borrowed money. When interest rates soared out of sight, our projects developed serious cash flow problems as we struggled to pay the escalating interest costs. My investors were hurting, and they looked at me as the source of the pain: I had brought them in. For 18 months, I didn't sleep.

What I had to do to get out of this mess honorably was emotionally gut-wrenching, technically complex, and could probably take up another book. I managed to get about 90 percent of their investment back to my investors, at a time when other investors in similar deals were losing everything. I kept my credit. I kept my reputation. I kept my business integrity. What I didn't keep was my $1.8 million. When the dust cleared, I had lost it all. I was going to have to start over . . . again.

*Almas, in a photo taken by Tariq. "She hasn't
smiled like this since he died," says Tasreen.*

I lost something else during this period: my marriage. The business problems were not the only reason Almas and I decided to separate, but they didn't help. They probably kept me from recognizing and working on distant, early warnings of trouble ahead. Several years of constant travel and uncertainty also took their toll.

The bigger issue we had to face up to was that we really hadn't known each other as well as we had thought. I frustrated her with my restrained style, which ended up not being a good match with her more emotional personality.

Almas has said we just got married too young. In addition to not knowing each other, we didn't know ourselves well enough. Her view is that we didn't have the personal tools and skills to hold the marriage together, and she's right.

I wrote my parents a lengthy letter explaining why we had decided on a divorce. I told them we felt we were constantly *patching* the marriage—and if it required that much patching, it wasn't built right in the first place. I told them we had decided to stop putting all that energy into patching, and to do what was right and necessary. I asked for their help.

At one time Almas blamed me for the breakup; at one time I blamed her. It is a source of happiness to both of us that the days of blame are gone, and we are now in the days of friendship. We were able to help each other, and maybe even lean on each other, as we struggled with the loss of Tariq.

In 1981, my life hit bottom. My money was gone. My professional career was a disaster. My marriage was over. My spiritual life had been shoved aside. I had no home. I moved to Atlanta to take a job I didn't want, because I saw no other options. I was living in a nondescript apartment in a strange city with no friends or family around me. I didn't look too great, the result of too much smoking and too little exercise. My health grew fragile. If someone sneezed in the next county, I caught a cold.

In 1983, I met a woman who helped me return to a healthy lifestyle. Glenda was just what the doctor ordered: active, successful, healthy in body and mind. I used to kid her that she had only two bad habits: water and milk.

Four months after we became involved, I stopped smoking and started exercising. The first time she got me to go jogging, the best I could do was a coughing, wheezing 100 yards. I thought I was going to drop! But I kept at it, and by the time I left Atlanta for San Diego, I could run 10 miles. Our relationship has mellowed to one of deep friendship, and the commitment I have today to exercise and physical health is really a gift from Glenda.

As I wrestled with building a new road for myself, I realized my business failures had taught me valuable lessons. I pondered how to use this hard-won knowledge. With no investment capital of my own, buying new businesses was not feasible. What made sense was selling my experience and analytical skills to others— if I could convince them that I was still a credible adviser. I decided to try to establish myself as a financial consultant. I certainly had at least one strong calling card: I knew lots of things people *shouldn't* do.

With vigorous prospecting, eloquent selling, and some good luck, I was able to land initial clients and bootstrap a new consulting practice. Over the next several years, the practice slowly grew, and I began to regain some optimism that I could succeed once again in the American marketplace.

In 1987, I received a major consulting contract from a San Diego-based client. I had been in San Diego before and liked it. I had another active client only 90 miles north in Los Angeles. I had always thought I would enjoy living in southern California, and now the idea made business sense as well. On January 1, 1988, I moved into an apartment in San Diego. Happy New Year!

I felt I had traveled far down a rebuilt road. I wasn't affluent, but I was financially on the mend. My consulting practice was solid and growing, and I was developing a reputation as a savvy and credible investment banker in my client circles.

For the first time in years, I looked OK and felt healthy. I was meditating regularly, and reconnecting with my spiritual roots. And now I was getting ready to set up shop in the lovely, cosmopolitan, seaside city of San Diego.

Among San Diego's many charms is the presence of a large Spanish-speaking community. I love learning different languages. As I got established in my new hometown, I enthusiastically threw myself into learning some Spanish. I'm now passably fluent.

One of the benefits of my travels has been the enjoyment of communicating with different people in different languages. In addition to English and Spanish, I speak Swahili; the Indian dialect called Kachi; Gujarti, another Indian dialect; Hindi; and Arabic (which I use mostly for prayer)—each with varying proficiency. I'm not great at any of my "second languages," but I relish opportunities to use them.

———————

Perhaps the most difficult part of this period had been learning to live apart from my children. I visited them in Seattle whenever I could. It wasn't often enough. I missed them, and they missed me.

When Tariq was 14, he wrote himself a letter that made me realize how much he had grown.

He was struggling with friendship issues.

He was discovering that although he was not big, he was a good athlete. He was fast, agile, coordinated, able to compete in wrestling and track.

His heart had gotten its first roughing up on the road to romance, at the hands of a girl named Jessica, and it had turned him philosophical.

He had established his first concrete set of life goals.

Here's an excerpt from the letter:

> I feel this year is going to get a lot better. I feel that my attitude has now changed. I feel that nobody is worth the pain of a broken heart. I'm going to tough it out.
>
> This year I also have a few goals My goals are to achieve a 4.0, and gain a respectable spot on all my varsity sports. I have a goal to somehow leave a mark at this school. I want people to remember me by something very important. I really want to kick butt this year in everything I do. I'm going to stop moping around. I want to be the best in everything I do. I want to go to Lake Washington High School and leave a mark there, too. I will then continue on to Stanford. I will get my Ph.D. and become a brilliant lawyer.
>
> Most of all this year, I would like to get over Jess for good.

Ambitious career aspirations. Romance problems. I can relate, son.

As Tariq grew older, our relationship took contradictory turns. He wanted to know more about me. He wanted me to get to know him better. He wanted more "face time" with me, more emotional intimacy.

The contradictory part was that as he approached his late teens, the face time we did have was often a source of irritation to him. I began doing the classic father-to-son thing: putting pressure on him to start charting a career plan, and making it clear that my preference was for him to follow in my footsteps and become a businessman. I would have enjoyed mentoring him and working with him.

Since he had practically no interest in business, this was a source of conflict between us. His love was art, especially photography. It was clear we had different visions for his life path, and he was confident and assertive enough to look me squarely in the eye and tell me my vision for him was not his idea of a good time. Almas is scrupulously honest about everything, even when it's to her detriment. I think Tariq inherited some of that.

In 1992, Tariq graduated from high school in Seattle and moved to San Diego. He had been accepted at San Diego State University. During his early years, travel and then divorce had been obstacles to our being together. Now, finally, we would again live in the same city. We hoped to truly get to know each other. We wanted love and mutual respect to wash away the effects of past bitterness and current differences. We were ready for our relationship to mature and thrive.

We both wanted these things, but it still wasn't easy. Often it's not for fathers and sons. I had a hard time putting down my expectations and plans for Tariq, and letting him live his own. And it was very hard on him to feel that I was disappointed in him.

I understand completely how I made him feel that way. But in fact, I never was disappointed in him. I have always believed you can't be good at something you don't like. The important thing is not how lofty the work, but how well it's done. The message I *wanted* to communicate to both Tariq and Tasreen was, "Whatever work you do is OK, but not to do it the best you can is a waste. If you sweep streets, be the best sweeper."

In October 1994, Tariq wrote me a letter: an honest, articulate communication, straight from his heart, telling me what was going on inside. Here's part of it:

Dear Dad,

The last two years of my life in San Diego haven't been easy. I thought I was here to go to school, meet my father, and possibly follow in his footsteps. Tempting though that was, following in your footsteps is not for me. Because I've tried to live up to those expectations, I haven't been able to be honest with you, and in return, I believe you haven't been honest with me. There is something great in you, for I've seen touches of it, but for us to be who we are, there has to be total honesty.

By trying to live up to these expectations I've gotten down on myself and stifled what attributes I possess. I wanted to make you proud of me, but something inside wouldn't let me. I have to be myself, and the only way to do that is by putting our relationship on the line.

I have to be honest with you, and accept the fate of that stand. I don't want to know your fake side, your businessman, formal Azim. I want to know you: your hates, your anguish, your loneliness: the stuff that makes a person who he is. I think I'm the one to help you. I

*think you've always stayed far away from anyone that
would.*

*For me to move on with my life in a positive
direction, I have to take control, deal with my mistakes,
grow—and not be scared of wrecking your expectations.
I love you, Dad, and want to be a part of your life, but
not as the son who will live up to your standards. I think
you're trying too hard to be perfect. This I can't be.*

*I do realize at this point in my life I can't make it on
my own, financially, mentally or emotionally. I
appreciate your help. I know you have honest intentions
and a good soul. Why else would you be giving me a
chance in what seems to you an unworthwhile
endeavor? Do what you feel is right, it's the only way.*

Tariq's career direction—art, photography—was so very
different from mine. I was *called* to be a businessman. I was
studying balance sheets in accounting school in London when I
was 19. I did have difficulty understanding and accepting his
choice. But I never felt it was "unworthwhile." I knew I would
be proud of his accomplishments.

What I didn't know was that we would only have three
months after he wrote his letter for me to be able to show him
that.

I would gladly have supported him through college,
whatever his major. I was proud of the work ethic he had already
developed. His sense of personal responsibility drove him to
earn some of his own money. He took a job delivering pizzas to
do it.

———

Everyone travels a road. We all have stories to tell about how we've gotten where we are. But we're shaped by more than places, events, family and relationships. We're also defined by our beliefs, our spirit.

Let me conclude this chapter by talking about the Ismaili faith. It may be that the truths of that faith, even more than the events of my life, have determined the path I'm on.

The prophet Muhammad, the founder of Islam, died in the year 632 AD. After his death, there was disagreement among his followers about who should succeed him and assume the mantle of spiritual leadership. There were also differences of opinion regarding issues of law, worship and ritual. Muslims split into two camps: the Sunni and the Shiites.

The Sunni are by far the larger group, comprising 85 percent of the one billion Muslims throughout the world. (Many people may not be aware that only about one-fifth of Muslims are Arabs.)

Shiite Muslims believe that Muhammad's son-in-law, Ali, was the rightful successor to Muhammad. Shiites have formed many different sects, and the Ismailis are one of those. The North American Ismaili population of about 100,000 is one of the smaller Ismaili communities. There are many more throughout the world. When my family moved to Vancouver and then Seattle, we were the first Ismailis in the Northwest. As others moved there, our home became the first Ismaili mosque in the area.

As with many religions, Ismailis have prevalent cultural characteristics and values, as well as shared faith. It is fair to say that Ismailis tend to be pragmatic, frequently have a flair for business, and are inclined not to get hung up on form over substance. Education is highly valued, as is scientific and intellectual achievement. Ismailis often have a multinational orientation, which enables them to adapt to and become part of widely diverse locations and societies.

Ismailis also accept their responsibility to work toward a better, more peaceful world. Volunteer service to our community is expected of us, and is a backbone of our faith. In 1986, the Aga Khan signed a formal Ismaili constitution which became binding on all members of the faith. Two clauses of this constitution provide direction which is clear and important:

> . . . *To seek cooperation and friendly relations with all other peoples*
> . . . *To make an effective contribution to the societies in which we live*

Ismaili faith emphasizes a rational, thoughtful approach. We recognize and honor the authority of our Imam. But we are encouraged to use our own minds and intellect to understand our world, our lives, our spiritual journeys and the will of God.

The Qur'an is the book of Islamic faith, our equivalent of the Jewish Torah or the Christian Bible. Properly interpreted, the Qur'an helps us penetrate hidden meanings. It contains hints, symbolic expression, and allegorical guides to higher meta-physical truths.

There is also a powerful, mystical component to our faith, something beyond formal rituals and external expression. We are invited to extend ourselves into a dimension of profound, inner mysteries, to gain new insight and understanding of our purpose and our relationship to God. It is to this dimension that we must transport our minds to grasp the concept of the universal soul of which we are all a part: you, me, Tariq; all who are, all who have been, all who will be. This mystical path of Islam is called Sufism. I have always been drawn to it.

A potentially explosive element in our world today is the increase in religious fundamentalism. This is not unique to Muslims, but there has been widespread media coverage of fundamentalist Islamic activities and sects. In some ways this is unfortunate. It has led much of the public, perhaps especially in the United States, to believe that Islam is inherently a dangerous and violent faith. Nothing could be further from the truth. One of the meanings of the word "Islam" is "peace."

A sadness we share with our brothers and sisters of other faiths is that violence has been done by Muslims in the name of Allah and Muhammad, just as violence has been committed by Christians in the name of Jesus, and committed by others in the name of God. This is terribly wrong. It does dreadful disservice to the faith. It distorts the great truths the founders of their faiths taught.

The truth is: the vast majority of Muslims, Christians, Jews and people of all faiths want peace.

I have discovered in myself a strong drive toward justice. My faith requires me to reject violence and work against it, to vigorously pursue justice and work to achieve it.

Perhaps that's why I embarked on the path I chose. Tariq's death initially turned me inward, toward hopelessness. But I needed to turn outward. Toward hope. Toward faith. Toward light, for myself and for everyone I could reach. To give meaning to Tariq's life and his death, I had to reach out.

And hold fast,
All together by the rope
Which God stretches out for you
And be not divided among yourselves
And remember with gratitude
God's favor on you
For ye were enemies
And He joined your hearts
In love, so that by His grace
Ye became brethren

Qur'anic Ayat (3:103)

Reaching Out

A solitude is the audience-chamber of God.

Walter Savage Landor, *Imaginary Conversations,*
"Lord Brooke and Sir Philip Sidney"

On Friday, April, 7, 1995, I drove to Mammoth Mountain in northern California, on the eastern flank of the Sierras. I needed to be alone for a few days. I hoped the solitude would help me calm my inner storms.

In the 10 weeks since Tariq's death, life had lost all motivation. I was moving through my days like a zombie. For sanity's sake, I had to come to terms with the horror of losing Tariq, and chart a course that would bring meaning back to my life.

I fought my way through the Los Angeles Basin freeway traffic, and finally made it to the relative calm of Highway 395. I drove north past obscure towns with wonderful names: Adelanto; Kramer Junction; Randsburg; the neighboring towns of Cartago and Olancha; Owenyo; and just before my destination, the welcoming, homey sound of Tom's Place.

Traffic on 395 was so light that at times the road seemed like mine alone. The solitude was soothing. My only company was an audio cassette: inspirational reflections of Deepak Chopra. I thought he might point me in the direction of solace.

When you're hot, you're hot, and when you're not, you're not. At one point during the drive I went to change cassettes in my car's tape player. I swerved slightly, crossing the line. My car was virtually the only one for miles, so it seemed like no big deal. But the key word is "virtually." The one other car in the area was driven by a member of the ever-vigilant California Highway Patrol. He observed the swerve. Quiet communing with Deepak crumbled under the force of reality. My drive toward restoration and healing started with a traffic ticket.

A friend owns a condominium in Mammoth Mountain, and he had graciously encouraged me to use it for a few days. I arrived toward the end of the day, unpacked, and headed out to a local restaurant for a light dinner of grilled Cajun fish and salad. The staff at the restaurant were practically the only humans with whom I exchanged words for the next four days. After dinner I stopped at the local store, picked up a few groceries for my retreat, and headed back to the condo.

The condo had a nice fireplace. A stack of firewood lay outside, ready to provide warmth and light. I brought in a few logs and lit a fire. I gazed at the tongues of flame. They shape-shifted and danced. I willed my body to relax. My thoughts shifted and danced with the flames in the fireplace: ephemeral; starting, stopping, turning in unpredictable directions.

I should have spent more time with Tariq. How could I have been so busy? He was diminutive in size, only about 5'5", but he had a spectacularly thick head of hair. I remembered how I used to love to run my fingers affectionately through all that hair. Sometimes I did it in public, to his vast embarrassment.

I recalled the last time Tariq and I had been together: January 9. We had met at 10 o'clock for breakfast at our favorite restaurant, the Hobnob, in the Hillcrest section of San Diego. We both loved breakfast. The Hobnob serves great breakfasts.

When Tariq was growing up, our favorite breakfast was steak and eggs. Over the years we had both gotten health-conscious, and didn't eat much meat anymore. But when we got together for breakfast, we always reverted to our early, shared enjoyment of carnivorous cuisine. We had broadened our tastes, though. This particular morning, corned beef hash sat in for the steak as accompaniment to our eggs.

I had recently returned from a trip to India. Before I left, he had asked me to bring him back a rug, preferably a green one. I searched in every city I visited, and finally found just what I was looking for in Agra: a bottle-green rug. It was gorgeous. I took it to the restaurant and gave it to him that morning. He loved it.

(One of Almas' sisters had a dream involving that rug. In the dream, Tariq had told her to tell Jennifer that the day she wanted to connect with him, Jennifer should just sit on the rug and meditate. After Tariq's death, I told Jennifer she could keep anything she wanted of Tariq's belongings. The first thing she asked for was the rug.)

We brought each other up to date on what was going on in our lives. Even though he wasn't interested in business, Tariq was always eager to hear about my adventures in the fast-paced world of American enterprise. He was insatiably curious about my deals and activities, and had a computer-like memory for details. He never forgot a thing.

After I filled him in on my news, it was his turn. He told me his relationship with Jennifer was going great and getting stronger all the time. He was enjoying his art and photography, and was seriously considering leaving San Diego State to focus on what he really loved. He didn't think the formality of college education was necessary to his artistic growth.

Jen had a good friend in New York. They were thinking about driving back east to see her when the heart of the winter had passed, and the weather was more hospitable. They were also going to check out New York as a possible relocation destination. Tariq had never really turned on to southern California. He thought it was plastic and hedonistic. He wasn't sure it had much of a value system.

The meal together had been a delightful interlude.

Impossible that it had been less than three months ago. More like three lifetimes. Impossible that we would not see each other again in this life. But we would not. Impossible, too painful to bear, that I would never tousle his hair again. But I would not.

As I thought about Tariq's fate, I began to think about Tony's. He was in jail, still more than a year away from the "conversion" of his sentencing statement. Something had gone terribly wrong if a 14-year-old could become a casual killer. What was it? How had we let it happen?

I thought about a man named Ples Felix. I knew his name, and that he was Tony's grandfather. I hadn't met or talked to him. His grandson was alive and my son wasn't. But Tony's prospects for anything but the grimmest of lives were dim, indeed. In a real sense, Ples and I were both robbed of our children that fateful night. America lost two of her sons. For what? How many more had been and would be lost for no reason? For the sake of us all, shouldn't there be something we could do to save those lives?

I reflected on stories I had seen and statistics I had read about youth violence in our country. I had paid absolutely no attention to them. Why should I? What did they have to do with me?

Now they had everything to do with me.

The United States is arguably the greatest of all nations. But a child is arrested here for a violent crime every five minutes. Guns on the streets of the United States take the life of one of our youths every hour and a half. It chilled me to think of how many parents were wearing the same cloak of grief I was. Where were our priorities?

We have such wealth, such ability, such achievement. Each week we push back daunting frontiers. We look to the ends of the universe through our telescopes. We stretch technology to communicate instantaneously anywhere in the world. We penetrate the secrets of the atom, the depths of the ocean. We design and build massive construction projects in miraculous time frames. We transplant organs and end Cold Wars. With some readjustment in priorities, couldn't we add "stop kids from killing other kids" to our impressive list of accomplishments? Wouldn't it be worth trying?

So much of the world looks to America as an example, a leader. Is this killing the example we want to set, the leadership we want to offer?

Questions, questions. So much easier to come up with than answers.

———

Some of my best conversations happen when there's no one around but me. I can't run and hide. "Ah, but what have *you* ever done about the problem?" I asked myself. "If you start pushing to make things better, you might hit something uncomfortable: maybe change has to start with you."

The Aga Khan has always emphasized that we must balance the material and the spiritual. And he has made it clear that Ismailis must be good citizens in any society they join. I didn't think I had been terribly out of balance—or a bad citizen. But "not bad" might not be the same as "good enough." If I were going to campaign for changes in social priorities, I had a premonition it would involve taking an excruciatingly close look at my own.

It could never again be "business as usual" for me.

———

I had tea and fruit for breakfast each morning, then went out to do some skiing. The demands of the vigorous exercise allowed me to move my focus from mind to body for a few minutes—a brief but welcome relief.

After lunch I took long walks. The solemn purity of cold air and white snow lay in peaceful contrast to my inner churning.

Evenings were spent in the condo reading, gazing into the fireplace, deep in thought. The fundamental question I kept coming back to was: how do I get through the rest of my life? How do I live with the agony of having been cheated out of sharing my son's life?

I was grateful that Tariq and I had gotten through our disagreements, that our relationship had been in a good place at his end.

My thoughts drifted again, to the teaching of the first 40 days of the soul's journey. I knew he was at peace, even though I was not. An understanding began to grow: to find peace for myself, I needed to find something I could do for him, for his journey. The grief had to be broken—or at least set aside—for both our sakes. Grief alone could not give meaning to his death. Something good had to be done, and it had to be done in his name, inspired by him. The phrases "spiritual currency" and "fuel for the journey of the soul"—the teachings of the wise man who had helped us through Tariq's funeral—kept playing in my mind . . . and it was in my friend's condominium in Mammoth Mountain, in front of the fire on a chilly April night, that I got the first inspiration about what I might do.

What if I became a foe: not of the boy who killed my son, but of the forces which led him to kill my son? What if I reached out as far as I possibly could, and devoted myself to fighting the plague of youth violence?

It bucked me up a bit to finally ask questions I might be able to answer. Dwelling on questions for which there were no answers had left me feeling defeated. I started to think about what might work.

Most Ismailis devote energy to volunteer activities in their communities. I had led and participated in many charitable efforts to benefit Ismaili groups and needy people in other countries. Maybe my next efforts should focus on what was happening outside my own front door.

My community could be the starting point, and should be, but it would not be the ending point. Even with this tragedy, I marveled at the love I felt for my adopted country. With the sudden surge of energy which often accompanies a powerful new idea, I suddenly wanted to fight the good fight everywhere in the country. It was overambitious and melodramatic, but it was how I felt at the moment.

The first inkling of what was to become the Tariq Khamisa Foundation had been born. It was as if three strands of longing came together to form a slender lifeline: to do something for Tariq; to do something for my country; to do something for myself.

I spent the rest of my time at Mammoth Mountain focused on this idea. For the first time since Tariq's death, I felt the slightest return of my old energy. I saw the first glimmer of a reason why my own life should continue.

———————

I returned from the mountains to San Diego feeling that at least I had left my status as a walking zombie behind. Clearly, the quality of the rest of my life depended on my reaction to this tragedy. For life to have quality, it must have purpose. Without purpose we're just aimless collections of molecules, and that's what I had been for the last couple of months.

At this time, the controversy over whether to try Tony as an adult was at its peak. A petition demanding adult status for him was being publicly circulated. Of course it had no legal standing, but its supporters gathered 1,400 signatures.

I was not very keen on the idea that trying a 14-year-old as an adult was the answer to our problems, but I felt hesitant and uneasy about interfering in the legal proceedings. I decided I had to leave that to the authorities. My focus was going to be on future violence prevention, not past violence punishment.

I started writing down ideas and initiating conversations with just about everyone I knew. I told them about my concept for a Tariq Khamisa Foundation and its mission: turn Tariq's death into a force for good and find ways to protect other children from the same fate. I'd ask for their views, their suggestions—their involvement. I knew I couldn't do it myself.

Success would require the collective energies of every person we could get to participate.

The response was incredible. Practically everyone was willing to do something.

My friend and "older brother" Dan Pearson quickly agreed to help. He has a natural ability to figure out what needs to be done, in what order, to accomplish objectives. Sal Giacalone, the owner of DiMille's restaurant, said we could count him in. Dan's wife, Kit Goldman, a woman of extraordinary energy and creativity, pledged her support. Gary Hardke, a member of the law firm of Hillyer and Irwin, agreed to handle the legal issues that accompany the establishment of a nonprofit organization. I was filled with gratitude at the reception these people, and so many others, gave to the idea for the Foundation.

The months of July, August and September were filled with the planning, communication, and resource hunting required to launch a new effort of this kind. Once I got started, I returned to my old habits of working insanely long hours. But my previous work had been about economics and financial success. This was much more important.

After months of hard work, we were ready to start. On October 26, 1995, a meeting took place at my residence. About 50 people were there. These were the key individuals who had committed themselves to our mission. We wrestled with the physical laws of time and space, and managed to fit all 50 into my modest townhouse. Once everyone was coffeed, introduced and seated, the meeting started. The Tariq Khamisa Foundation had been born.

Peter Deddeh was the prosecutor from the District Attorney's office who had been assigned to Tony's case. His work gives him a clear view of the impact of youth violence on our society. He has supported what we set out to do from the beginning. That night he gave the opening speech. Several other people spoke. Then Dan introduced me.

Everyone there already knew the facts about what had happened to Tariq. Choked with emotion, I managed to share with them my inner feelings and journey, and to thank them from my heart for their promise of commitment and work on behalf of our children. Mine were not the only tears shed that night.

———

In the midst of all this activity, starting a month or so after my return from the mountains, another feeling came and stayed. I found it occupying more of my thoughts. I chewed on it, and eventually made up my mind.

After the meeting at my home was over, I took Peter Deddeh aside. I asked him if he could do something for me. I told him I wanted to meet Ples Felix.

———

As a prosecutor, Peter Deddeh has dealt with many situations involving grievous family losses and the accompanying emotions. "Everybody deals with that experience a different way," he says. "I've adopted a policy of respecting any way a victim's family chooses to handle the death of a loved one. But in my experience, Azim's handling of this situation was unique.

"I had gotten to know Ples pretty well before Azim made the decision to meet with him. It happened mostly during the time of the hearings to determine whether Tony was going to be tried as an adult.

"Tony's defense attorney called Ples to the stand to testify at the hearing. Through the defense attorney's questioning, and through my own, a picture of Ples emerged. He impressed me as a man of high standards, of great character, of concern for his grandson and for all young people. Ples himself had overcome a lot to get where he was, which also impressed me.

"Those hearings were a painful time for Ples. He had to come to court day in and day out, and listen to the bad deeds and shortcomings of his grandson. And much of the hearing focused on the time Tony lived with Ples, and their relationship. Tactically, the defense started by trying to paint Tony as the victim of his grandfather's harsh discipline. But when Ples got on the stand and spoke about his and Tony's life together, they sort of backed away from that. Ples was obviously a very 'squared away' person, and the discipline he had provided came across to everyone listening as consistent, fair—even loving.

"I think what happened was that, initially, Tony had told the investigators that his grandfather hit him sometimes, and was harsh to him sometimes, and left it at that. So as defense attorneys sometimes do, they extrapolated that out to mean he was an abused child, and Ples was an overly heavy-handed disciplinarian. But when Ples got on the stand, everyone could quickly see he was no ogre.

"For a while, though, he got a lot of unfavorable media attention, and that was hard on him. If he had been reluctant to meet and work with Azim, it wouldn't have been hard to understand why. He'd had enough exposure to realize he risked getting microphones and cameras stuck in his face, and people asking him things like, 'Well, wasn't Tony living with you when he pulled the trigger? Why did he do those things when he was with you?' He didn't have to open himself up to reliving what his grandson had done. He didn't have to risk resurrecting those demons and getting scalded by the limelight again. But he did, because that's who he is.

"Then I got to know Azim over the following few months, and saw much of the same character in him.

"If Azim had come to me the day after I got the case and said he wanted to make an overture to the defendant's grandfather to work together, I certainly would have been shocked. But having gotten to know them both, when Azim finally approached me about taking this step, I really wasn't surprised. I saw the connection.

"Azim is thoughtful and deep. In some ways, I might say he thinks with an Eastern mind. That might be a somewhat different perspective on the world, and on life and death, than the typical Western cultural viewpoint.

"As Azim did, I also have one son. I don't think I could have put myself in Azim's shoes, and taken the path he did, if my only son were killed. I understood what he wanted to accomplish, and had great respect for it. I could not have handled the situation with the same grace and dignity he displayed. He rose above the bitterness."

Peter's comment about my "thinking with an Eastern mind" is probably true. I feel very fortunate that I have an Eastern heritage, that I was born and grew up in Africa. I have stayed true to my Eastern roots, through family and faith. But I feel equally fortunate to have spent the last 25 years in the Western world, and the United States in particular. One of my goals in life has been to combine the spiritual wisdom of the East, the material wisdom of the West, and the soul of Africa.

———

The day after the meeting at my house, Peter called Henry Coker, Tony's attorney, and told him I wanted to meet with Ples. Henry told Peter he would be happy to discuss this with me. Peter arranged for us to go to Henry's office on Friday, November 3.

Mike Reynolds, writer and filmmaker, was invited to come with us. He had been deeply moved by Tariq's story, and was heavily involved in getting the Foundation started. On November 3, I picked Mike up, then swung by to get Peter, and the three of us went together to Henry's downtown office. I realized Henry might think my desire to meet with Ples was a little unusual. He might even be worried about my motives. I was prepared to give him a full explanation of why I wanted the meeting, and what I hoped it might accomplish.

I was not prepared for what I saw when we entered Henry's office. Henry was seated behind his desk. And lo and behold, sitting opposite Henry—there was Ples.

———————

Mike Reynolds would later say, "The second Azim walked into the room, and he and Ples looked at each other, the hair on the back of my neck stood up. I knew something special was about to happen. There was such power in that moment. It was like a circuit closed, and somehow positive forces were poised to flow from a terrible tragedy. To witness Ples and Azim shaking hands was an amazing experience. The father of a slain child shaking hands with the grandfather of the killer? It doesn't happen!

"But to have these two men come together and accept that a tragedy had happened at one moment in time, and be prepared to move on from there together, was a spiritual moment like nothing I've ever experienced."

———————

My first reaction was simple shock, because I hadn't known Ples was going to be there. I think I actually took a step back before we shook hands. Then we all sat down. Ples wears his hair in dreadlocks. That day he also wore a colorful African-style cap, almost as large as a turban, with his suit and tie.

After Peter made a few introductory remarks, I began to tell Ples why I had wanted to meet with him. I told him I wanted him to know that I did not have any feelings of revenge toward him or his family. We both felt the grief of having lost a young life. I told him about the work we were going to undertake through the Tariq Khamisa Foundation, to fight the plight of youth violence that had wounded us both so severely.

Mostly, I just wanted to reach out and connect with this man as part of my healing process. I had no idea what his reaction would be. I had no expectations.

Ples took my outstretched hand with no hesitation. He offered his condolences to me and my family with bedrock sincerity. He told me he wanted me to know that my family and I were in his prayers and meditations every day. This struck a deep, responsive chord in me, because of the importance of meditation and spirituality in my own life. It created an instant, powerful bond.

That bond was to stay with us, and provide a mutual source of energy for the commitment we were to share. I felt from the beginning that here was a good man.

Ples said he would pledge to help in any way he could with the Foundation's work. I was very moved by this—partly because I took an instant leap forward and realized what he might face. At every appearance or meeting, he could be seen by some as the man who had been the guardian of the killer, and therefore partially responsible for what had happened. I could not help but admire his bravery.

———————

"The first thing I noticed in that meeting," Peter Deddeh recalled, "was that both Ples and Azim were extremely respectful toward each other. They were deferential to each other's loss. Azim made it clear he saw Tony's situation as a great loss for Ples' family, and Ples communicated those same feelings about the Khamisa family's loss of Tariq. There was an unusual amount of warmth.

"My work revolves around legal conflict. It is adversarial by nature. In my profession, we get used to sizing up opponents. When we meet other lawyers during cases, although it's collegial in some respects, we're always looking past appearances and trying to figure out where this person is really coming from. We're thinking, 'What does this tactic mean?' or 'What does that statement mean?' Our training gives us that perspective.

"But what came through to me so loud and clear during this meeting was the complete absence of those dynamics between Azim and Ples. They took each other at face value. They were open to each other. There was no stiffness, no sizing each other up. It was comfortable, natural—surprisingly lacking in tension and stress.

"What makes this situation unique is that on both sides of this tragedy you had people who were so articulate and insightful. Then they reached out their hands to each other.

"Azim is not a Christian, but what he did struck me as the ultimate act of Christian forgiveness."

Ples said later, "When I heard that Azim Khamisa wanted to meet with me, my first response was a great feeling of relief. It seemed like an answer to my prayers. I had felt so strongly that I wanted to meet face to face with Tariq's family and express my sympathy for their tragic loss. And I wanted to offer myself to them, in any way that would help. As soon as Henry told me of Azim's overture, I asked him to make it happen.

"That first meeting was powerful for both of us. Based just on what I had read about Azim, I had formed the impression that here was a man of spirit, a God-loving man. All his comments in the media had demonstrated such love and compassion. And on meeting him, all those impressions were confirmed. I felt I was looking into the eyes of a person whose soul was there for me to see and touch. The bonding was instantaneous. Within a few minutes, I knew we would be lifelong friends.

"Azim told me of his desire to start a foundation in memory of his son, to develop programs to prevent youth violence. I told him to count me in. The idea of working with him so others would not have to experience our grief resonated very deeply inside me.

"I was coping with terrible pain, on two levels. I had lost my one and only grandson to prison, and that grandson had been responsible for the death of Azim's one and only son. Azim showed me the road to healing by inviting me to work with him on something deeply meaningful.

"As we talked, in my mind and in my emotions, I could feel the shroud of pain start to lift. I felt a new focus of positive energy. I realized we had the potential to not only help heal each other, but perhaps contribute to the healing of people we didn't even know.

"In my life experience, I've always carried some of the spiritual base I inherited from my parents. I don't claim affiliation with any specific church denomination or religion. But I feel fellowship with others all over the spiritual globe.

"I believe we're all children of the one God, and we all have within us a spirit that is created, maintained and driven by the will of God. That understanding has gotten me through a great deal. Everything that has happened is a part of God's will for my life, and tragedy is a part of the great test we are all put to. Every test, every tragedy, creates an opportunity for us to work through a process of healing, and invites us to strive for excellence to benefit more than just ourselves.

"For this tragedy to end up having positive meaning, rather than being an obscene monument to waste and destruction, we had to find a way to do something enduringly good. What better path for us to seek than to simultaneously honor Azim's son and devote ourselves to saving other children!

"Azim and I come from very different backgrounds. Yet we were able to forge partnership and friendship under some of the most difficult circumstances imaginable. I believe that's because we both chose, even under the shadow of tragedy, to think along the lines of love, forgiveness and compassion, instead of following the path of blame, hatred and anger. We both chose to do what we could to break the cycle of violence, not add to its flames."

Ples Felix is an eloquent, compassionate spokesman for the Foundation. He calls the work "a ministry."

At the conclusion of the meeting in Henry's office, I told Ples that we would be having a second Foundation meeting at my house the following week. I asked him if he would be willing to speak to the group, and he said he would.

At that meeting, my parents—Tariq's grandparents—were there. Tariq's mother Almas, my ex-wife and good friend, was there. Tariq's aunt Neyleen, my sister, was there. Tariq's sister Tasreen was there. Tariq's cousin Salim Nice was there. When Ples got up to speak, he was looking into the eyes of the people who had loved Tariq Khamisa. I can't imagine a situation more delicate or emotionally charged than the one Ples willingly faced at that meeting. He concluded his speech by saying,

> *What can we do to prevent these tragedies? We must commit to support anything which promotes the precious value of our future: our children. The Tariq Khamisa Foundation is such an effort. I will commit to this effort!*
> *Will you?*

After Ples finished, I gave my speech. When we were done, there were virtually no dry eyes in my house. My neighbor, Bonnie Trotter, wrote a check to the Foundation on the spot, becoming our first donor.

That day, it was my hope that we had taken the first steps in a thousand-mile journey.

Reflecting on that day, Dan Pearson says:

"I am still struck by the memory of Ples walking—alone—into a room filled with 50 people, all of them Azim's family, friends and colleagues. When Azim's father got up to meet Ples, the room fell almost silent. There was tension; uncertainty. No one had been part of a situation like this before: a grandfather about to get face to face with the grandfather of his grandson's killer!

"Azim's father walked over to Ples, greeted him—welcomed him. As they shook hands and started talking, Azim's father placed his other hand on Ples' arm. It was a gesture of such grace: grandfather of one lost grandson to grandfather of another.

"With that gesture of good will and peace, Azim's father took the tension out of the room. At that moment, I think we all suddenly felt the true meaning of forgiveness.

"Throughout the evening, each member of the family spent a private moment with Ples. Each exhibited the same sense of kindness and acceptance.

"I'm sure Ples' stomach was churning, but he entered with grace and courage. He had to realize he was in an extraordinary situation, and he conducted himself impeccably. His speech was so appropriate: not so much what he thought, but what he felt. From the heart.

"The burden of what Tony did is heavy on him. But this was the start of the resurrection of Ples Felix.

"What enabled Ples and Azim to come together was their shared spirituality. They have different faiths, but they both believe that life is forever."

———

Programs require resources. During November and December, we were focused on determining what resources the Foundation could develop for our work. By the end of December, I felt drained by the long hours and the emotional impact of the work we were starting. I needed to "water my roots" at their source. I returned to Africa to visit family and friends. I came back feeling refreshed, stronger, ready to complete the Foundation's startup phase.

In April 1996, we were able to hire the Foundation's first full-time employee: Brian Horsley, a talented young man with boundless energy and commitment to the TKF mission. Office space was donated by the Hillyer and Irwin law firm. The local CBS affiliate had picked up the story of the Foundation, and had given it substantial news time. We had momentum, community support, enough funding to get us started, our first staff member, and an office. We were ready to begin our work.

If we see the world as inherently evil, there is no reason to believe it can improve. But if we see that the forces for good in the world are, at the very least, on an equal footing with the forces for ill, there is great hope for the future.

M. Scott Peck, *The Road Less Traveled & Beyond: Spiritual Growth in an Age of Anxiety*

"You Do Have a Choice"

In a world where children carry guns
Tender hearts grow harder every day
Were they ever their father's loving sons?
Oh Lord, please help us find the way

Kit Goldman, *Tariq's Song*

On July 10, 1996, shortly before 9:30 AM, students of Birney Elementary School in San Diego began filing into their school auditorium. Their clothes and faces mirrored the increasing diversity of our public school system.

I enjoyed the mix of jeans, coveralls, T-shirts, sleeveless shirts, and shirts with an impressive array of variations on the theme of stripes. Shirts and blouses were tucked in, shirts and blouses were hanging out: the full panoply of American grade school sartorial statements.

At 9:30, Kit Goldman stood in front of the group, turned on the microphone, and thanked the children and school staff for inviting the Tariq Khamisa Foundation to be with them that morning. Our first program was about to begin.

We were at Birney Elementary by invitation of the school counselor, Carol Roblauskas. Carol sensed that trauma relating to Tony Hicks' story was growing on the campus. Some of the children had known Tony. Many more had heard of him and his involvement in Tariq's murder. Buzz was building among the students, particularly when Tony's guilty plea and sentencing were generating massive amounts of media attention. The students were confused: What was good? What was bad? What was true? What should they think about their former schoolmate? Carol felt an urgent need for intervention, and called us.

Carol's request was the trigger for our newly assembled team to leave the realm of high-level objectives and begin the hard work of concrete program development. We had been invited to meet with hundreds of children. An opportunity was in front of us. What, exactly, should we say? How should we say it? What format would work? Who would lead the program?

We were blazing new trails, looking for new solutions. Blank pieces of paper can be exhilarating—and a daunting challenge. We spent long hours exploring concepts, hammering out ideas, testing different approaches.

Everyone contributed. But the core idea for what we settled on came mostly from the creative mind of Kit Goldman. It follows an effective group training approach she has pioneered with her consulting company, Live Action Edutainment. The program format includes a facilitator, a diverse guest panel, concise presentations, and audience participation and interaction via a roving microphone. It combines elements from classrooms, talk shows, executive training seminars, and live theater.

We called the program the Violence Impact Forum. Its goal was to send a simple, powerful chain of messages to young people: the impact of violence is terrible and irrevocable; violence is a *chosen* behavior; making that choice brings grim consequences; alternatives are always open.

Kit started by telling the group who Tariq was, and what had happened to him. The fact that Tariq had been shot by Tony Hicks had personal impact on these students. Tony had sat in their classroom seats, walked through their halls. This story was not theoretical, distant, out-in-the-ozone stuff. It was all too near and immediate.

Kit told them we wanted to share thoughts and get their perspectives on the turbulence and tragedy of youth violence. She explained that the people from the Foundation were there to be resources. Then she introduced Ples and me, saying, "I want you to take careful note of the fact that these two men are sitting together." She also introduced Mike Reynolds. While interviewing Tony in prison and documenting his story, Mike was trying to be a mentor to Tony.

Then she introduced Kevin, a former gang member. She explained that Kevin had made some bad choices, but then had decided to put them behind him and make some good choices. He wanted to share both good and bad with these kids, so they could benefit from the wisdom yielded by his trip down a very rocky road.

The students in the audience had had a recent taste of death. A classmate had drowned after being swept out to sea. Kit expressed her condolences for their loss, and emphasized the difference between a death caused by nature and one caused by human choice. "By the time you leave here today," she said, "all we want is for you to be thinking about your own lives. All we want is for you to take that critical moment before you take action, and think about what it means, and we hope that by doing that, you're going to make good choices."

Then Kit called me to the microphone. "There's nothing in the world more precious than a child's life," I started. And suddenly, I couldn't go on. Despite the fact that I was getting used to standing in front of groups and speaking, I had to stop. Floating through my mind, against the backdrop of all these young, priceless faces, was the face of my own son. Tears welled up in my eyes. A giant hand gripped my throat. All I could do was to stand there, waiting for my voice to come back.

Finally, I was able to continue. It felt like 5 minutes had gone by, but it was probably only 10 seconds. "To me, a child's life is more precious than even my own. You see, I know this from personal experience. Seventeen months ago my only son Tariq was shot and killed. He was delivering a pizza. I'll never forget answering the phone and hearing that my son was dead. At first I could not believe it was true. But after I talked to his girlfriend, Jennifer, the truth began to sink in. He was gone— gone forever. I would never see him or touch him or hear him laugh again.

"I didn't know how I would be strong enough to call my daughter and tell her that her little brother was dead. I'm sure most of you have little sisters and brothers. Just imagine what it might feel like to get a call like that. I felt helpless and paralyzed. You see, I'm the father. My job as a father is to keep my children safe. And I wondered, what could I have done? Before that phone call it seemed impossible that this could happen, even though I've seen violence in Africa, where I was born.

"It seemed impossible to me that four teenagers would surround my son to try to rob him of a pizza, and that one of them would shoot him dead for a pizza. I felt numb for weeks. The pain was too great."

I looked at the audience to see how they were reacting to my remarks. I was trying to take complex issues, and make them accessible to grade schoolers. Would I be successful? The kids were quiet, attentive. Much less fidgeting going on than one would expect from a group of that age. In fact, they seemed riveted. I was encouraged.

"When my feelings slowly started to come back," I continued, "one of the first things I felt was anger. But mostly my anger was at our country, our society, for not doing anything to stop more and more children every year from killing and being killed.

"With the death of my son, I felt my life had lost all its purpose. I was angry at America. I thought about running away to another part of the world. But I realized I loved my adopted country, and I had to stay and fight. I had to face reality. But how?

"This is where you children come in. Sometimes we all get caught in situations where others do things we can't control. That's how it was with Tariq's murder. But if you think about it, we do have control over how we respond. *We always have a choice.* You see, I *chose* to turn my grief into positive action.

"I couldn't help Tariq when he was ambushed and shot. But I could do something in his name. I could fight back. I could try to save others from experiencing the nightmare of youth violence.

"In our country, every 92 minutes we lose a child to a gun. That's 16 children a day we lose to a gun, every day! And on both ends of the gun there is a tragedy. That's why I decided to reach out to the family of Tony Hicks, who pulled the trigger on Tariq, and Tony's grandfather, Ples Felix.

"Ples told me of his daily prayers and meditations for Tariq and the Khamisa family. And now we work together, as you can see. Talking to children just like yourselves, in the hope that we

At a Violence Impact Forum

Above: Ples and Azim

Left: Azim and Brian Horsley, the Foundation's assistant executive director

can say something or do something to keep you from choosing violence.

"Reaching out to Ples was not an easy thing for me to do. Many people thought I should seek revenge; get an eye for an eye. But what would that accomplish? Would it bring Tariq back? It would only continue the violence that took Tariq's life. Answering violence with violence won't change anything.

"All you boys and girls here, you all deserve to be able to walk without fear. You deserve to have your dreams come true. To raise families of your own. You deserve . . . a *future*. We adults of this world have done a pretty lousy job of making that happen so far. We need you to help us. Will you do your best to help stop violence?"

I paused and looked around at the audience. They looked at me intently. There was no immediate response; just the tension and energy of complete attentiveness.

"Do you all promise to try?" I asked. I paused again. I wasn't looking for a mechanical or superficial vocal response. I wanted the question to sink in. I wanted them to think about this. I wanted them to start an internal process that maybe, just *maybe*, would help them make a good choice one day when high stakes were on the line. I heard a resounding, "Yes!"

"I hope that you do," I finished. "God bless you." I walked over to Ples, and we hugged each other—a simple, powerful symbol to show the children friendship and unity in our mission.

I had given these students deep, emotional issues to consider. And I had addressed them not as children, but as intelligent, perceptive people who could grasp what we were trying to communicate. Would the communication succeed? No way to tell at the moment, of course. But it might have as much chance of succeeding as if I had been addressing adults. After all, it's adult leadership that has set the stage for this plague of youth violence. I figured these kids couldn't help but understand at least as well. Maybe better. They don't want to kill. They don't want to be killed.

Then Kit introduced Ples to the group. He was wearing a big blue T-shirt, not tucked in, and blue jeans. His long hair was pulled back. With his beard and his glasses he looked like a hip, gentle poet. His opening words reflected the deep spirituality which is so much a part of this man.

"First of all," he said, "I need to give praise to our Creator for allowing us to be in this room together in good health and good spirits. I'm glad to look around and see all your beautiful faces.

"The second thing I need to say is, God created you perfect. God created each one of you with love and compassion. And those are strong qualities that exist in you. Sometimes we forget that. It's important that you understand that you're born with strength of character. You're put on this earth for a purpose that's guided by the will of our Creator. That moves you forward in life. *The responsibility you have as you move forward is to make choices.*

"Some choices will benefit you in life. Some will create consequences. You have to learn to understand the difference between acts that create positive outcomes, or benefits, and those that create negative outcomes, or consequences. Let me explain.

"Most of you have heard about my grandson, Tony. He attended this school. He came to school like many of you, challenged by the prospect of confronting education. Tony was a kid who didn't like to read very much. He didn't like to spend much time studying. He would rather be playing and having a good time, as most kids would.

"However, Tony did work very hard while he was at this school, because at one point he was held back and had to repeat fourth grade. That was very difficult for him. He really didn't want to. But he worked hard. And encouraged by his teachers, his counselors, me and his mom—people who loved him—he was able to skip out of fifth grade into sixth grade and graduate with the rest of his class. And that was based on the choice Tony made to work real hard and be successful in fifth grade. He wanted to be the very best fifth grader this school had ever seen.

"And his work was rewarded. That's a choice that had benefit for him.

"Much later in his life, at age 14, Tony made another choice. And this one had consequences for him. He decided it was more important for him to hang out with people who were gang members than to interact with people who were about more positive activities and behaviors. He made a choice one Saturday morning to leave home, even though he had never had any problems at home.

"The only things required of him in our home were that he study in school; that he take care of and exercise his body, his mind and his spirit; and that he keep his room clean. Those were the only things required of Tony.

"But those proved to be difficult things for him. They caused him to pursue other choices. So instead of being bothered with homework, exercise and chores, he decided to run away. All I found was a note.

"I was shocked and distressed. For the first time since my grandson had been with me—five years—he was not at home. I didn't know where he was. I had no way of contacting him.

"That Saturday evening, after calling the police and filing a report of a runaway child, I sat in horror and shock at a late-breaking television news story. It was a special report, informing the city that a 20-year-old San Diego State University student who had been delivering pizzas was shot and killed in North Park. I have to tell you, at that moment I had a very bad feeling come up all over me. Because it was the first time since Tony had been with me that he wasn't in his bedroom, asleep, by 9:00 in the evening. It was the first time since he had been with me that I didn't know where he was. I had no idea.

"I was heart-struck and panic-stricken. And as a former Green Beret who fought in Vietnam, I don't panic easily. But this was my grandson, a kid who meant everything to me. He is as close to a son as I'll ever get in this life. But I didn't know where he was!"

Ples paused and looked at the children. They were transfixed. He didn't have tears in his eyes as I had. But the anguish was not far behind his soft voice, filling in the spaces between his words.

"And after three days passed," he continued, "with some work and some effort by the authorities, Tony was finally brought into custody—*but still as a runaway*. It wasn't until later that same evening that a police detective told me that Tony was charged with the murder of Tariq Khamisa.

"I don't know if any of you have ever lost anyone. But when you hear that you have lost someone because they made a decision that resulted in the death of another person—none of that can be taken back. None of it can be undone.

"But we do have to understand the consequences of the choices that Tony made.

"When he decided to leave home, he made a choice not to be within the protection of his family.

"When he accepted a handgun from an 18-year-old who said, 'We're gonna commit this robbery'; when he received and carried out the command from this 18-year-old to shoot another person; when he pulled the trigger; once the bullet came out and took the life . . . the choice was made, and it could never be undone.

"At that point, the life of Tariq Khamisa was no more. A precious life snatched from this planet—gone! At the hand of a 14-year-old kid who had dreams of being a scientist. Because some 18-year-old kid told him to shoot.

"So there was a series of poor choices that Tony made. And all of those choices have resulted in consequences he will have to live with the rest of his life. Most of you know that Tony was sentenced to 25 years to life in prison. And he's a 15-year-old kid now. *He's going to be locked up longer than he has been alive on this planet.*

"He'll be 37 before he's eligible for parole. He should be going to school, learning skills, learning how to socialize, learning how to drive a car, learning how to work. But he is locked up in prison because of poor choices.

"And what we emphasize to you as young people is that you are perfect; you are beautiful; you are precious. And you want to make the kind of decisions that will benefit you during your life. But, too quickly, many of you will say, 'That won't happen to me—*can't* happen to me.'

"All of us who knew Tony knew it wouldn't happen to Tony—*couldn't* happen to Tony. And then we were so shocked. We still can't believe this is the Tony we knew.

"But the Tony that was home with me was not the same Tony standing in the streets, hanging out with gang members. That was a different Tony.

"And many of you may be two different people: a private persona that's you when you're at home with your people; and a public persona that's you when you're with your friends on the street.

"But whether you're at home or on the street, *make the right decision for yourself.* Make the choice that's a nonviolent choice. Make the choice that keeps you and your friends out of harm's way. If you're not doing that, you're not a friend.

"A friend takes care of a friend. A friend takes both the benefit and the responsibility of friendship. And if you're not doing that, and if your friend is not doing that for you, *then you are not friends.*

"Be friendly to yourself. Make choices that will benefit you, and benefit your life. And remember that anyone who tries to convince you to do harm is not your friend!

"Stay well and God bless you."

———

Kit turned the microphone over to Mike Reynolds. "Rojo," as he is known to his friends because of his orange-red hair, is a burly, outgoing filmmaker and writer who has dedicated a great deal of time and energy to helping us tell Tariq's story.

"I spent a couple of hours with Tony at Juvenile Hall last night," Mike started. "And Tony wrote something he wanted to give you today. He also wanted to tell you that what happened to him, he never wants to happen to any of you. In a minute I'll read what Tony wrote.

"But first I want to tell you that Juvenile Hall stinks—and Juvenile Hall is the nice part of the system! CYA [California Youth Authority] is worse, and adult prison is worse than that. Juvenile Hall is steel and cement. No windows. You are locked up behind that door, and once it slams, you're there alone. You get no hugs at night from the people you love. *You are alone.* And that is what Tony is living with right now. And this is what he wrote to you kids here at Birney."

> *Hi. A lot of you kids may have seen or heard of me, or know me. I went to this school from the fourth to the sixth grade. I'm in the ninth grade now, so I'm not much older than most of you. I'm a 15-year-old boy—serving a prison sentence of 25-to-life.*
>
> *I did a crime that I regret and that I'm ashamed of. When I first moved to San Diego from L.A., I needed friends. So I joined a gang. We didn't do much in the gang but hang out with our friends and have fun. I didn't stop to think of the people I was hurting while I was having fun. I just had fun.*
>
> *I was arrested when I was 14 for something I thought was going to be fun—until someone died. Now I see that what I was doing wasn't fun. I should have listened to the people who really cared about me—not the people I thought cared. You kids shouldn't need to have fun the way I did. Because it ain't worth it. It ain't worth 25-to-life. It ain't worth hurtin' the ones you love. It just ain't worth it.*
>
> *Thank you. I'm Tony Hicks.*

Then Mike played the videotape of Tony's sentencing statement to the judge.

Kit came back up. She had tears in her eyes. "It'll take you a moment to get through what you just saw," she said, her voice trembling. "It takes time for me, too.

"Let me ask you a question. Are there times when you feel that you *don't* have a choice? That you're going to *have* to do something wrong—because you have no choice? Is there ever a situation like that?" she asked, carefully scrutinizing the audience.

She approached the children. Leaning over, she picked a boy in the third row and extended the microphone to him. "Tell me what kind of situation that might be," she encouraged the boy.

"Well, like, if someone's trying to beat you up," he gulped out. The kids giggled.

"OK," Kit said. "When you're getting beat up. Any other time you might not have a choice? Peer pressure? Is that a problem?"

A blond boy, about nine years old, raised his hand and came up to the microphone.

"Or when somebody puts a gun to your head," he said, "and tells you to kill somebody else or beat someone up." My heart sagged, feeling suddenly as if it had been transmuted to lead. This boy, these children, should be thinking about getting ready for their next baseball game—or at worst (from their perspective), their next history test. How terrible that they must think of guns and death. How terrible that we must work so hard to protect them from guns and death.

"Choices," Kit was saying. She turned to Kevin, the former gang member. "Kevin, you've had some choices in your life. Suppose someone puts a gun to your head and says 'shoot someone else or I'll kill you.' Or suppose someone's about to beat you up. What about that?"

Kevin stood up and took the microphone: a good-looking young African-American man, whose calm, straightforward demeanor gave little indication of his tumultuous past.

"You guys are lucky," he told them. "You have a school, our Foundation, a counselor who cares about you. If you need someone to talk to, they're here. When I was in the fifth and sixth grade, and I was a gang member, I didn't have a lot of choices like you have.

"Violence was a way of survival for me. I didn't feel I could call a counselor or the Foundation to say, 'I need help. I don't want to hurt anybody. Can you get me out of this gang?' There were no resources. But now there are.

"Because of what happened with Tony Hicks, a lot of people are trying to reach out to you. And I am, too. I was a gang member. And I have some things I want to tell you.

"First, I want to talk about nonviolent choices. I now have two daughters of my own in school. They're about the same age as some of you. And I don't want them to be where violence is.

"Violence will destroy all your dreams! I had a dream once that I was going to be a firefighter. But now that I've got a prison record, the chances of my ever being a firefighter are not good.

"For those who like to play games: if you play the violence game, they've got a place for you. I just left it. It is not a fun game to play. So you have to say 'no' to violence. Look at me! I had a dream. But I got into gangs."

One of the girls in the audience asked Kevin why he went to prison.

"The first time I went to prison, it was me and a group of my friends. I *thought* they were my friends. Just like Tony. I was living with my uncle, and not listening to him. He told me to stay in the house one night. I didn't. I had to go out and hang with my friends. We committed armed robbery that night. So I went to prison. For 3 years and 10 months."

"How old were you?" one of the children called out.

"I was 13," Kevin replied. A murmur went through the audience. He could have been one of them. "If you commit adult crime," he warned them, "you're gonna do adult time."

"What gang were you in, Kevin?" another voice called out.

"I was in the neighborhood Crips," he responded. The "Crips" are a well-known gang, among the most violent.

Kit didn't want to let that pass. "Does that impress you?" she asked. "Kevin, is that impressive?"

"NO, it's not," he responded emphatically.

———

Toward the end of the Forum, Kit asked if anyone had any questions. One of the students came up with a dandy: simple and right to the heart. "I have a question for Mr. Khamisa," a girl of about 12 said. "Did you dislike the family of Tony when you found out he had killed your son?"

"No," I told her. "I was angry, but I was angry at America, because we had failed to give better options to some of our children. Instead of some of you being gangsters, I think all of you can be heroes. And that's what we're hoping to make happen through the Foundation.

"One of the reasons the Foundation has reached out so well," Kit added, "is what you see here: Mr. Khamisa and Mr. Felix sitting next to each other. Could you do that if someone you love was taken away? Could you answer nonviolently? Think about it. What would have been gained if Azim Khamisa had responded with violence? Would that have helped the situation? Would it have brought Tariq back? But now, because of how he responded, something good can come out of the tragedy of Tariq's death."

Then another girl of about 12 or 13 asked another great question: "Why do people wait to make a Foundation until somebody gets killed?"

"Young woman," Kit answered gravely, "that's a very good question. You know what? We just didn't know. Life is a learning experience, and maybe the test is that once you know enough, can you change?"

At the conclusion of the program, the student counselor faced the audience. "I hope you heard this morning what I heard," she said. "It's about choices. And the point is that you *do* have a choice."

————

The results of this, our first program, were astounding to us. The interest and attention from the kids, the response from the teachers and administrators, the letters we received afterwards, sent us a forceful message. Clearly, we had touched something vital, and were on the right track. The challenge would be to develop what we had presented into a flexible, repeatable program. This would require effort and funding.

————

A month before, on June 1, 1996, I had given a speech to a bigger crowd than I ever expected to see, much less address. The occasion was the "Stand For Children" rally at the Lincoln Memorial in the nation's capital. Marian Wright Edelman, president of The Children's Defense Fund—the main sponsor of the rally—had heard of the Foundation and the work we intended to do, and invited me to be a speaker.

Here is the brief speech I gave to 250,000 people and a host of television cameras which broadcast the rally live.

My name is Azim Khamisa. I speak to you as an international businessman, a proud but impatient citizen, but foremostly as a father. It is 16 months and 11 days since I lost my only son Tariq. He was 20 years old.

When Tariq was 18 he wrote an essay about his philosophy of life. He believed that one should live by giving, treat others the way you want to be treated, and give life your best effort.

The 14-year-old boy who killed Tariq had no such philosophy, and when Tariq refused his demands, he pulled the trigger. That night, America was robbed of both children.

I ask you: how is it that in this great country, children too young to have a driver's license are not too young to have a gun? Why spend billions on Desert Storm or conquering space when every day, in our own backyards, defenseless children are wiped out in a frenzy of bizarre violence? Why can't this powerful nation get its priorities right? When did we begin to accept these killings? Why do we let these killings continue?

The Old Testament view of an eye for an eye is not the answer. Trying 14-year-olds as adults is not the answer.

I founded the Tariq Khamisa Foundation to help turn my grief into positive action. Working against the forces which resulted in Tariq's death brings quality and purpose back into my life.

From the beginning, I felt there were victims at both ends of the gun. After much reflection, I made the decision to reach out to the family of my son's assailant. I met Ples Felix, the grandfather of Tony Hicks, who pulled the trigger on my son, Tariq.

Ples told me that the moment he learned Tony was charged with Tariq's murder, all the promise, all the future plans he had for his grandson crumbled. He said, "I wept and prayed for Tariq, and for Tony."

Ples has since joined the Foundation, and we work together to save lives of the young people of our community, and all across the country.

*My family and I have been gratified by the community support we have received. But this support must not come from any sense of obligation to me personally. I have already lost my only son. The real obligation is to your children, grandchildren, and other young ones who have not yet been stricken. Believe me when I tell you, **our children are not safe**.*

After the rally, Marian Wright Edelman told her friend Aileen Adams about the Foundation. Aileen was the Director of the Federal Office for Victims of Crime (OVC), a part of the Justice Department. In late June, she called the Foundation and had a lengthy discussion with Brian Horsley, the Foundation's assistant executive director, about our plans and directions. She mentioned some upcoming events in which she might want us to participate.

Subsequently, we received a call from one of Aileen's lieutenants, inviting us to be part of an event sponsored by NOVA: the National Organization for Victims Assistance. NOVA is an umbrella organization for victims' rights advocacy groups. The event was their yearly conference. We agreed to attend.

When we arrived, we were greeted with an unexpected request: they asked if I would deliver the keynote address at their "Victims' Tribute Breakfast." I said yes, and Brian, Dan and I hurriedly started working on a speech.

The speech went well. It gave us the chance to connect with members of the OVC staff, and to share the Foundation's plans with them. They were enthusiastic and encouraged us to apply for a discretionary grant. We did, and eventually it was approved, giving us the funding to expand our outreach and continue our program development.

March 6, 1997. Tariq's birthday. How wonderful it would have been to take him out for a celebratory dinner. But fate had spoken. His birthday must now be recognized in a different way.

That morning we presented another Violence Impact Forum. This one was at Roosevelt Junior High, a school with a substantial number of at-risk students. We did five assemblies: four in English, one in Spanish. Over 1,000 students attended. That night we also offered a Forum for parents, to provide an opportunity for them to hear and discuss these critical issues.

After the Forum, we had a very special event: a tree-planting ceremony. We wanted to leave behind a permanent symbol of life, growth and beauty. Aeriaka Jacobs, the school's assistant principal, gave a brief introduction. "Today you have heard that we need to be responsible for the choices we make.

There are always positive and negative consequences to choices. So take your time and make the choices that will affect your life positively.

"The planting of this tree symbolizes hope. I hope that each time you pass by, and see it growing with flowers around it, you will be revitalized. I hope you will be inspired to make friends and build commitments, not tear them down."

Then she invited one of the students to come up and read a poem called "Dependence." This young man had probably never read anything in public in his life, much less a poem. He gave great feeling and sincerity to his reading. The first verse of the poem is a wonderful message to us all:

We can't play alone in the game of life
We're dependent, my friend, on others
We can't get by in the struggle and strife
Except with the help of our brothers.

Then Aeriaka, the young poetry reader, and Kit donned work gloves and prepared to start planting the tree. San Diego Mayor Susan Golding came to the microphone.

"This occasion is testimony to the incredible human spirit of two men," she said, looking at Ples and me. "It demonstrates something we rarely see: true forgiveness, true understanding, and the willingness to reach out.

"I am hopeful that the work of the Foundation will save the lives of children. Some of those children we don't know yet. And some may be here with us today.

"In honor of the memory of Tariq Khamisa, and the Foundation's pledge to work to reduce youth violence through education, I proclaim March 6, 1997 to be Tariq Khamisa Day in

San Diego. His day will be commemorated by this tree planting ceremony. And I hereby recognize the Foundation and its many volunteers for their commitment to increase awareness of youth violence, seek its causes, find solutions, and present educational programs that are understood by children."

She walked over to the planting area: a square of soil approximately eight feet on a side, in the middle of a large expanse of concrete.

"You've got good clothes on, Mayor Golding," Kit said good-naturedly, "so I'll do the digging." Kit prepared a hole in the dirt and handed the mayor the flower seedlings to be planted around the tree. The mayor took one and placed it in the hole. One of the Roosevelt students took a trowel and began scooping dirt. Her hands and the mayor's—different colors, different ages, working together, inches apart—made a stirring sight.

"May it grow forever," the mayor said when the flower was successfully laid in its new home.

Ron Roberts, chair of the San Diego County Board of Supervisors, addressed the crowd. He recited some statistics with startling impact about the increase and severity of youth violence. "We hope the Foundation's work can change these statistics," he said. "We applaud their efforts to help assure that young people have a chance to grow into healthy, successful lives." When he finished, he was invited to wield a trowel and plant a flower.

Two members of the school's ROTC brigade, in full uniform, brought out the tree in its pot and carried it to the planting square. "This white orchid is our tree of life, of abundance, of growth," Kit said.

A Roosevelt Junior High School student helps San Diego Mayor Susan Golding plant a flower. Kit Goldman oversees the work.

The school's ROTC brigade carries the white orchid tree to be planted in Tariq's memory.

Ples Felix and Louis Simpson, the father of Solomon "Solo" Simpson, came forward to say a brief prayer and participate in the planting.

Kit thanked Michael McGee from California Governor Pete Wilson's office for attending, then invited my family to step to the microphone. Almas recited an Islamic prayer from the Qur'an in Arabic, and Tasreen followed with the English translation. "Give us a life of peace," the prayer asks.

I thanked the school for working with us to present a program on Tariq's birthday. Then I read a passage from the Psalms:

> *Blessed are the men and women who have grown beyond their grief and put an end to their hatred. They are like trees planted near flowing rivers which bear fruit when they are ready. Their leaves will not fall or wither. Everything they do will succeed.*

I added my own prayer:

> *We ask that you grant us the fortitude to build an America that is safe for children. And we ask that you bless Tariq's spirit with eternal peace. Amen.*

The children came up, grabbed tools, and began digging dirt to plant flowers around the tree. Television cameras captured the faces of all races gathered around the planting square. With each trowel full of soil, they added fuel for Tariq's journey of the soul.

May the tree of life grow long at Roosevelt Junior High School.

After Roosevelt, we worked on refining our program. We created an in-class curriculum. We focused specifically on adding victim assistance elements to the program, and created a resource guide handout so youth, adults and school staff would know where help was available.

The in-class curriculum provides a guide for the presenting teachers. It includes a set of questions designed to identify the children's attitudes toward violence, personal safety, peer relationships, power, vengeance, and their plans for their lives. It guides them through the events, the people, and the consequences surrounding Tariq's shooting by Tony. A powerful video begins the presentation. Each key step of what happened is discussed and analyzed—at a level carefully matched to the age of the audience.

Whatever we try to accomplish in our lives, it's important to measure progress. That's often easier to say than to do. If you're teaching arithmetic, you can ask students to multiply 84 by 103, and either they can or they can't. Measuring attitude change is more complex. But our first pass yielded encouraging results.

In October 1997, we debuted the new curriculum, and used a before-and-after questionnaire. The questions were compiled by Kit Goldman with input from the University of California at San Diego sociology department, under Dr. Richard Madsen; and from Dr. Shelly Zablow, a prominent San Diego M.D. and child psychologist.

Revenge is a force which triggers endless, escalating violence—particularly when gangs are involved. Revenge is insidious. It emerges for real injuries—or just perceived ones. The results showed that after going through the Forum, there was a substantial drop in the percentage of kids who would seek violent revenge for a violent act.

A particularly promising statistic emerged when we asked, "If a friend told me that he or she was afraid of getting hurt or killed, I would . . ." and offered multiple choices. Before the Forum, 11 percent—33 children—chose the response, "Tell them to join a gang and get a weapon." After the Forum, only three chose that response, and on a subsequent follow-up questionnaire, none did.

The next step will be presentation of the program at several schools which have a substantial population of at-risk children. Elementary schools, junior high schools and one high school will be included. The schools are all within a three-mile radius of where my son was killed.

The tree and flower planting ceremony, the "Garden of Life," will be a signature part of the program. It's a sad fact that many students at these schools will have lost someone to violence. They will be invited to plant a flower in honor of their lost loved one. We will emphasize that the tree and the flowers are not just in memory of Tariq: they are also in memory of the departed who were dear to the children there.

At Roosevelt, I helped a Cambodian girl who had lost three sisters to violence plant three flowers—one for each lost sister. She was nine years old. As I handed her the jug to water her newly planted flowers, she smiled.

Most of these kids have never had an opportunity to touch potting soil, or plant a new flower or tree and watch it grow.

The first two times we did this, we had to rush out and buy more flowers because so many kids wanted to plant one. The ceremony is meaningful to them, perhaps even therapeutic. It's also a way of letting them participate in beautifying their daily environment. And in this era of tight budgets, most schools can't go out and buy trees and flowers themselves.

———

After we developed the core Violence Impact Forum curriculum, Ples Felix was asked to comment about the Foundation's progress toward its mission.

"The connection that the Tariq Khamisa Foundation is making with people will have tremendous long-term benefits," he said. "For children, and those responsible for children. I have very high expectations.

"I see a time when the Foundation will be a clearinghouse— and a teaching center—for important information about the safety and well-being of children; and for methods to keep them from being involved in violence, as perpetrators or victims.

"We've come a great distance in a short time, due to the high-intensity, deep-penetrating determination and dedication of the people involved. There's a shared vision of what the work is about. And every day we work together, the vision gets clearer.

"The Violence Impact Forum gets people's attention in ways that stay with them. It's not like looking at a commercial filled with buzzwords. It resonates deep in their spirits, and helps them understand the message being sent."

———

San Diego Deputy District Attorney Peter Deddeh offered a view of the big picture that's right on target. Asked for his perspective on the Foundation's work, he responded:

"There are lots of programs out there, lots of attacks on youth violence, coming from different quarters. There's not *one* solution, or *one* program or *one* thing. It's a multidimensional problem requiring many different approaches.

"The public tends to have a simplistic view, and sometimes thinks if we do *one* thing right, such as teach all the problem kids to read, we'll get less youth violence. Or if we mentor them all we'll reduce youth violence. But the problem has to be attacked from a number of avenues. Certainly, kids need to read and be mentored. But they also need other education, safe after-school recreational facilities, and safe homes to go to.

"The Foundation fills a certain niche. It's consciousness raising. You bring their program into schools to make kids confront the issue. Then you follow that up with other services that, once the kids' consciousness is raised, help them say 'Hey, maybe I should stay away from gangs. Because now I understand what tragedies gangs wreak on families and society—especially families.' In that sense, the Tariq Khamisa Foundation will be beneficial.

"But it can't be the be-all and end-all. They're not going to solve the problem by themselves. They're defining their niche, and once they do that, they'll be helpful. The real solution is many different people approaching the problem from many different angles. When you put together this mosaic of all the attacks on the problem, you reduce the problem."

Peter's observation about "many different people" being needed to solve the problem of youth violence reminded me of an op-ed article in *The New York Times* dated June 3, 1996. The piece was written by Bob Herbert after the "Stand For Children" rally. Herbert said:

> *The odds on the nation's future would look pretty good to anyone who took the time to stroll the area between the Washington Monument and the Lincoln Memorial at the height of the rally. It was a study in inclusiveness, the most thoroughly and comfortably integrated large crowd I have ever seen.*
>
> *It was a crowd that spoke—in its commitment, its decency and its variety—to the real possibilities of America. It was the way America might look if its promise were ever realized.*

The promise of America starts with its children. Many of us will have to be involved to realize that promise. But doesn't "*all* of us" sound better?

Join me, please.

> *With love our shattered hearts will heal*
> *And it's love that fuels the voyage of his soul*
> *But we'll have to feel pain we don't want to feel*
> *If we want our hearts to once again be whole*

Kit Goldman, Tariq's Song

Tariq Khamisa Foundation
Communities United Against Youth Violence

The mission of the Tariq Khamisa Foundation is to:

◆ create safer communities

◆ stop children killing children

◆ foster nonviolent choices

◆ cultivate personal responsibility through critical thinking and awareness

For more information, write or call:

The Tariq Khamisa Foundation
550 West C Street ◆ Suite 1700
San Diego, CA 92101-3568
Phone (619) 277-5700
Fax (619) 595-1313
e-mail: tkf1@juno.com *wrong.*

Toll Free: 1-888-HELP TKF   (1-888-435-7853)

The Foundation is a 501 (c) (3) nonprofit corporation.

Other People's Bardos

*Anyone looking honestly at life will see that we live in a
constant state of suspense and ambiguity. Our minds are
perpetually shifting in and out of confusion and clarity. If
only we were confused all the time, that would at least
make for some kind of clarity. What is really baffling
about life is that sometimes, despite all our confusion,
we can also be really wise! This shows us what the
bardo is: a continuous, unnerving oscillation between
clarity and confusion, bewilderment and insight,
certainty and uncertainty, sanity and insanity.*

Sogyal Rinpoche, *The Tibetan Book of Living and Dying*

Death claimed Tariq before he had a chance to make his mark
on life. We can only guess what he might have achieved. I do
know he loved children and wanted a big family.

I'm his father. I'm biased. I think he would have done marvelous things.

But marvelous or not, each of us leaves our prints on the
minds and events we have touched. We're an interconnected
web. We shape others and they shape us back. Sometimes we
know these others. Sometimes we don't, and never will. Some
are dear; some are strangers. Once we start tremors along the
tendrils of the web, who can say where they will end?

In this chapter, four people share insights born through Tariq's death. The lives of Brian Horsley, Dan Pearson, Kit Goldman and my daughter Tasreen have been changed because they decided to join me on my crusade. That participation has caused them to look deeply into their own lives and beliefs. Their stories are part of my story.

So are the voices of some of the children we've touched.

And finally, my life path has been redirected and made to cross the paths of other people on journeys begun by violence— most memorably on the remarkable day that 16 of us came together in our nation's capital.

————

In December 1995, Brian Horsley was within four months of receiving his bachelor's degree from the University of California at Riverside. He had some serious decision-making before him: what direction should he chart for his career?

A slender, athletic San Diego native, sporting a crew cut held over from his Army days, Brian radiates health and energy. He relates to the challenges faced by the kids with whom the Foundation works because he vividly remembers his own tough times as a teenager.

Here's how Brian reflected on joining the Foundation, and the experiences and observations that have sprung from the job:

"My core interest was to get into some kind of community service," he recalls. "Preferably something involving kids.

"My first idea was a program the San Diego Chargers football team might use to benefit local youth. I met an ex-Charger who agreed to help me develop and present the idea. We got it in front of their public relations executive, but it didn't go any further.

"That was fortunate. At that time, the board members of the Tariq Khamisa Foundation were starting to define the requirements for a full-time assistant director, because Azim was getting swamped. My name came up.

"I had met Azim, but didn't know him well. When I learned I had been discussed as a candidate for the Foundation job, I was very interested. It sounded like a great fit with both of my career targets: community service and working with youth.

"I got together with Azim a few times for informal discussions about his vision for the Foundation, and what the job would require from me. We broke bread, got to know each other on a personal level. That was important. This is more than employment. I'm representing Azim's crusade and Tariq's name.

"Azim asked me to give him a write-up of my vision for a nonprofit foundation, so we could be sure our views were compatible. He needed to test my ideas, to make sure I had what a startup effort like this needed. He also asked me to write a letter about myself to the Khamisa family.

"We had a final meeting at which we reviewed the job description he had created. We spent a lot of time talking about how we would work together. Then we had taken the exploration phase far enough. It was time to decide if the partnership was right. He offered me the job. I said yes. We sealed it with a handshake.

"I'm still working based on that handshake. I've never received a formal offer letter. I can't imagine another situation where I could be comfortable without things in writing. But here, it works fine.

"I got my degree on March 23. Eight days later I was on the job at the Tariq Khamisa Foundation. Everything happened so smoothly that I never doubted it was meant to be.

"I don't think Azim's path following Tariq's death was so much a conscious decision as it was something inside him, something I call 'grace.' I don't think we see much grace in our world today. I think he was acting on something deeper than his conscious mind. Azim is not the most *religious* person I've ever met, but he's one of the most *spiritual*.

"Azim's grace-full path must have been a combination of his Ismaili faith, his mother's influence—she has a heart big enough to love the whole world—and Tariq's spirit. I think there was a voice inside Azim that was not his own, not of this world, telling him how to proceed. What he's done is just too far out of the norm in our society not to have been guided by some divine force.

"But it's the combination of Azim and Ples that makes the Foundation's message so powerful. The visual impact of seeing these two men together is so strong. I don't know of another partnership anywhere or any time quite like the one between Azim and Ples.

"We're where we should be now: focused and effective in one area of concentration. But I want us to be thinking about our future path as well—where we want to go, and how we're going to get there. Whenever I get the chance, I lobby for us to watch for opportunities to get involved in long-range solutions.

"It's difficult to measure this kind of work. But on a personal level, I tutor a couple of disadvantaged kids, and I've tried to be a mentor to one that I've known for some time. I hired another kid to help us here at the Foundation last summer, and I paid his salary out of my own pocket because the Foundation didn't have the money. I measure my own success by just being able to touch these kids' lives, help them get their grades up, help them tough out the bad things they have to deal with so they come through OK.

"About my personal feelings toward Tony Hicks: I'm ambivalent. I recognize that he did something wrong, and I believe you have to be held accountable for your actions, no matter what the circumstances. But I feel bad for the kid. I've probably seen the video of him over a hundred times. It never fails to make me reflect on how lucky I was to have parents who were caring and loving, who didn't beat me, who weren't addicted to crack. Tony got dealt a hand that was pretty bad. He was probably set up for failure the day he was born. But some have been dealt worse hands, and have still managed to make it through fine. I feel bad that it took this for him to understand some basic truths. I wish I had met him when he was 12, so I could have tried to help him out.

"If I had the power and the resources to make changes in our society so we wouldn't produce killers, I'd start with education. The system we've set up to educate our kids is a rotten, miserable failure. We spend so much money on it, and we don't get enough back. I'd slash the bureaucratic bloat, and get enough teachers so relationships can develop between them and the kids. We don't need to spend *more*. We need to spend *more wisely*.

"And it's education that determines the jobs people get: whether they're going to live comfortably or in poverty. We hear a lot of talk about the 'cycle of violence.' But there's also a cycle of lack of education: families where no one has graduated from high school, and kids are being raised without any value placed on educational success and achievement. Kids pick up on that. They behave accordingly.

"In my family, if you don't graduate from college, you're a loser. So everybody in my family goes to college. Maybe I wouldn't have that education today if it weren't a part of my family's culture.

"Looking beyond the specifics of Tony and the shooting of Tariq, our gun policy in this country is a tragedy. I'd outlaw guns that aren't specifically for hunting. I'd put a huge tax on ammunition—and spend it on education. I want to make it difficult for people to get the tools of violent death.

"I see racism everywhere, and somehow, we have to find a way to integrate neighborhoods. We must learn to understand each other and cherish the unique characteristics of other cultures. The more we see each other as neighbors, the better we're going to get along and the fewer problems we'll have. San Diego is heading toward a majority Hispanic population, so we'd better solve this one soon. If you asked the average white San Diegan if he knew he was standing on soil that belonged to Mexico up until his great-grandfather's time, do you think he'd know that? I doubt it.

"Maybe core racism isn't the problem. Maybe it's just the fact that we don't live close enough together. I don't live in a particularly great part of town, but the fact is, there are no blacks or Hispanics on my block—it's all white. And I think there's an implicit distrust of young, minority males that makes it hard for them to get hired into good jobs. If you walk around the building I work in, the window offices are white men, and the inside offices are white women.

"We have a 14-year-old black kid that's been doing some work for us at the Foundation. He's so proud that he can come down here and do something to earn some money. No one's likely to give this kid a shot at a good job. I've seen him walk down the street, and people are fearful of him. He's shy, quiet, intelligent. He doesn't get much family support to excel in school, but he's got all the potential in the world.

"But people fear him because he's a young, black male, and that's certainly going to be a part of his experience in the job market. When he applies for a job, if there's any other candidate that's as well or nearly as well qualified, they'll get the job over this kid. And that creates problems for us as a society.

"If there's a positive that emerged from Tariq's death, it's this: America is good at identifying problems and coming up with a range of ideas to try out. Then the ones that don't work are ruthlessly discarded, and we focus on the ones that do.

"This tragedy happened to Azim, a man it's 'not supposed to happen to.' And he moves among circles of people who get things done. He has caused the issues of gangs and youth violence to be brought to a different, higher level within this city; a level that may be positioned to effect real change and real solutions.

"In other words, we're not just preaching to the choir of the inner city people and the southeast San Diego people who already know the problems exist. Azim moves in the circles of La Jolla and Rancho Bernardo, and he can bring scrutiny of these problems to people who may not have been touched by them before. He can give them a heightened level of awareness that this can happen to anyone. And we're starting to see them get involved.

"Something else good may have come from this, although the connection is nebulous and I couldn't possibly prove it. In the last year and a half, since Azim started his crusade, there have been several cases where people charged with crimes said, 'That's it, I'm guilty,' where we wouldn't have expected that—

as did Tony Hicks. Perhaps we are beginning to create an atmosphere in which people are less willing to defend the indefensible; in which both sides are willing to work together to heal the damage. It's a concept called 'restorative justice.' And we may have fostered a process which makes restorative justice more possible.

"At least it's a start."

Pain, grief, loss, and ceaseless frustration of every kind are there for a real and dramatic purpose: to wake us up . . . and . . . release our imprisoned splendor.

Sogyal Rinpoche, *The Tibetan Book of Living and Dying*

The death of my son changed Dan Pearson's life almost as much as it changed mine. Deep runs our friendship.

Asked to think back on the bardo we entered side by side, he offered these thoughts:

"I lost a child in my twenties. I never talked about it. Thirty years later I'm in therapy. But if, God forbid, I faced that kind of tragedy again, the thing that would make me try to emulate Azim's response is that it has healed him—as much as one can be healed after losing an only son. And he has helped other people heal.

"I must admit, though, I've asked myself if I would have the courage to do it his way. I don't know. Even with the empirical evidence of the healing power of his path staring me in the face, I don't know if I'm that strong. And I didn't know he was either.

"When he turned around and responded to my comment about 'frying the bastards' with, 'I don't feel that way, there were victims on both ends of that gun,' I was numb. I looked at him, and probably had the same incredulous look on my face that everyone else did. I've always said that crisis builds character. That's wrong. Crisis *reveals* character. I saw a side of him I would never have known—and maybe he wouldn't have known, either—if he hadn't been tested by tragedy.

"I got involved in Azim's crusade to stop youth violence for a simple reason: he asked me to. He was my friend. I couldn't say no.

"But there's a very personal reason I've continued with it. I coined the phrase 'stop children killing children' because in another time, 30 years ago, I was a 25-year-old child. I pushed the woman I was engaged to marry in 90 days into an abortion. In a way, I now feel that I was a child who killed my own child. That's the deeper meaning for me of my work with the Foundation.

"Azim said he wanted to make a difference. When I saw the impact he was having, I thought, 'My God, maybe we *can* make a difference.' There's a crusader in all of us. The crusader in me said, 'There's a chance!'

"Here's an example of making that difference. After one of Azim's speeches, a woman in the audience stood up and said, 'I'm from St. Louis. I saw the article about you in *Parade* magazine. And I decided that day that if I saw two children arguing, I would never walk by that again. I would go over and say, "There's a better way to solve this problem." And I would become involved!'

"Other people said Azim talked directly to their soul. I've heard free-flowing testimonials like that all over the country.

"Marian Wright Edelman, of The Children's Defense Fund, cautioned Azim: 'Don't get too bogged down in a community-involved program. You have to trust that the awareness you are raising has its own life.' As a strategist for the Foundation, I'm trying to balance the need for us to have strong relationships in our community with the need to be a traveling road show, getting the message out to the widest possible audience.

"I grew up in the Midwest, where all those traveling preachers would come into town with a tent show. Everybody would go and get moved. Then the ministers would leave, and the people would get unmoved. But then the ministers got wiser. Churches got involved, and shepherds were there to gather the flock after the travelers left. Then church attendance always went up. We have to realize that unless we put people in place who will carry on the message afterwards, we can't be a successful traveling road show. We'll just be another piece of entertainment.

"Foundation work involves an inner process for me that's different from my work as a real estate developer. When I have a real estate meeting coming up, I grind and grind analytically to figure out what I'm going to say and do. Preparation for Foundation meetings seems to come more from inspiration. I open my mouth, and when I'm done, I think, 'Where did that come from?' It's a humbling experience, because it makes me feel that if ever I have been touched by the hand of God, it's now, steering me through this. Part of the reason I'm staying so involved may be that I want to see where God is taking me next.

"Driving back home from Azim's house the day after Tariq's death, I had a sudden vision of the next two years. It was a vision of dread, of horror. The Azim I knew would be gone. He wouldn't be able to laugh or smile—and I wouldn't be able to laugh or smile with him. Maybe it would be longer than two years. Some people never snap out of something like this.

"And very selfishly, I didn't want my friend, the guy I shared so many laughs with, the man I had come to love like a brother, to go away or to change.

"After Kennedy was killed, a quote from one of his friends stayed with me: 'Some day we may laugh again, but we'll never be young again.' That may be what this has done to Azim. I think the 'old soul' has taken over.

"But three years have passed now, and it isn't cloudy every day. The clouds are breaking a little.

"There are strong similarities between Azim's Ismaili faith and the combination of Hindu and Buddhism I follow. They both flow from a belief that life is forever. I think of the Ismaili faith as the 'thinking man's reincarnation.' If you start from that core belief, it changes the way you conduct your life.

"When I went with Azim to the funeral, I was struck by how 'out of order' this tragedy was. Sons are supposed to bury their fathers, not fathers bury their sons. But despite the fact that everyone was consumed with grief, not once, then or later, did I hear an Ismaili espouse an 'eye for an eye' feeling. There was no hostility. When they eventually arrested the boys, there was no applause; there was no 'By God, I'm glad they got those little bastards!' Good old Baptist that I once was, I expected that, but it didn't happen.

"There was great respect for Tariq's soul. There was recognition that a highly evolved soul had lived among them.

"When I die, I would like to have a ceremony like that, even if only 10 people showed up. It was so *healing*. What went through my mind was that if life *is* forever, this is the way to conduct the passing to the next phase.

"When I'm doing Foundation work, there's no inner certainty to assure me I'm making the right decisions. The work is new. It's scary. How *can* I be sure? But when I'm least expecting it, a 'here's what we ought to do' pops into my head. Sometimes I feel like I'm following the direction of the Carlos Castaneda character who said, 'Jump into the canyon, and trust the universe!' I believe I've been given a divinely directed mission, and I've never been on a divinely directed mission before."

———

The uniqueness and power of the bardo teachings is that they reveal to us, by showing with total clarity the actual process of death, the actual process of life as well.

Sogyal Rinpoche, *The Tibetan Book of Living and Dying*

———

In 1992, Kit Goldman embarked on her own bardo.

For 10 years she had been one of the mandarins responsible for the astonishing rebirth of the portion of San Diego known as the Gaslamp Quarter. The Quarter had been a classic inner-city skid row, a bad place to be traveling with your wallet after sundown. But its central location and colorful history gave it great potential. In the early '80s, the city decided to attempt resurrection.

City planners, land developers and an assortment of hard-charging entrepreneurs teamed up and went to work. A new landscape unfolded. Upscale condos replaced fleabag hotels. Boutiques and trendy restaurants occupied storefronts previously featuring Thunderbird in quart bottles. Well-heeled shoppers trod where down-and-out winos had patrolled, drawn by a massive, spanking new shopping center anchored by Nordstrom's. And Kit provided the area's cultural centerpiece by founding a live theater.

The Gaslamp Quarter Theater was the culmination of years of onstage and backstage work. It gave Kit an opportunity to do theater her way. For 10 years, as managing director and producer, she treated San Diego to an eclectic variety of stage adventures. Then her trademark restless energy kicked in. It was time to do something new.

In 1992 she turned the theater over to the management team, and founded a company to offer a new approach to industrial training. Live Action Edutainment combines Kit's theatrical experience with the latest techniques in interactive training. As we watched her fledgling company start and succeed, little did any of us know how important those skills would become in the fight against youth violence.

Kit was one of the first people I asked to join the Foundation's advisory board. When the time came to plan and deliver our initial program, the Violence Impact Forum, she was the clear choice to be the person in front of the audience, leading the program.

"The kids we talk to don't want to die young," she says. "They don't want to be outcasts. But there are times in their lives when they see no alternative to violence. And what we have to teach them is that even in the direst of circumstances, you don't have to seek violent revenge. We have to find a way to give life and reality to nonviolent alternatives.

"The key part of our outreach is to get them to think *in advance* how they'll handle a situation with the potential for violence. It's a horrible thought that Tony is younger than my own son—and in jail for God knows how long. One bad decision can lead to that. And they're more likely to make that bad decision if they feel alone. We have to show them they *can* reach out. There *is* help.

"One person with a strong enough commitment to principles can make a huge difference in our society. Laws alone haven't been enough. We need to get enough people committed as individuals to attain a 'critical mass' to stop all the wrong, all the violence. What Azim has done is unifying, transcending the barriers of race, culture and economics.

"Education is the key, and changes are necessary. We teach academic subjects, and we assume life skills will somehow be acquired along the way. Not a safe assumption! The curriculum has to include things like communication, conflict resolution, parenting, family dynamics, critical thinking, values, ethics.

"I'd like to ban the creation of gated, senior communities out in the desert. People need to stay involved! We need all the cross-generational relationships we can build. And I'd like to see elected politicians living in conditions similar to those of their average constituents.

"I would also like to see parents suffer consequences when their children are destructive. When I was in school kids fought, of course, but it was fists, not guns. What's changed is that children shape their view of the world with too much television and not enough adult supervision. It's easy to forget just how impressionable kids are. Movies and TV look real to them. When they see someone use a gun on the screen, it makes them want to use one, too. And they may not understand that when they do, death is real, not a movie.

"In some respects our culture has grown old and dysfunctional. Our whole country may be going through a bardo. The 'nuclear family' social model may be obsolete. Maybe we can't depend on it to raise our children anymore. But whatever will replace it is not here yet."

———

What distinguishes and defines each of the bardos is that they are all gaps or periods in which the possibility of awakening is particularly present. Opportunities for liberation are occurring continuously and uninterruptedly throughout life and death, and the bardo teachings are the key or tool that enables us to discover and recognize them, and to make the fullest possible use of them.

Sogyal Rinpoche, *The Tibetan Book of Living and Dying*

———

Early in 1998, my daughter Tasreen moved from Seattle to San Diego to start work at her brother's Foundation. Leaving Seattle was tough. She had grown up there and felt deeply connected. She had friends dating back to elementary school. She belonged to a mosque with 600 members—a valued spiritual community. She had landed a well-paying job after getting her college degree. And her mother, who is also her best friend, lives there.

She didn't want to leave. She left anyway, and is now my crusade partner as well as my daughter. I am thankful.

"My dad approached me in late 1997 about coming to work for the Foundation," she recalls. "I was dead set against it. I said, 'No way! I'm not leaving Seattle!' But Kit was also encouraging me to think about it, and I was involved in the VIFs. Every time I came down for a Forum, I felt my heart pulling at me. I kept thinking that if I did come down here, I could be more involved.

"My mind didn't feel ready to leave Seattle. When I first moved down, I called my mom three times a day because I was so homesick. I asked myself what I was doing here. But deep inside, I knew. I needed to be here. My heart wanted to be here.

"In college, I majored in sociology. My area of emphasis was studies in juvenile delinquency. That training prepared me for this kind of work, and I always wanted my career to be in something that was socially meaningful.

"When I graduated, I fell into the printing business. I did what many of us do: took the first acceptable job that came along. It was a paycheck. But after a while, it wasn't enjoyable, and it wasn't rewarding. When the time came, it wasn't hard to give it up.

"My objectives are to strengthen our volunteer program structure, and raise funds that will allow us to expand the geographical area we offer our programs in. But first, I want to see measurements come back that tell us we've really made a difference in our own community; that youth violence in San Diego has been reduced. Then I want to make our program available nationally. My dream is to reach kids all over the U.S.— anywhere we can do some good.

"My mother is an assistant teacher at a Montessori school in Seattle. The school has had a fundraiser for us the last two years—in January, the anniversary of Tariq's death. The principal of the school has been very touched by what we're doing. We send them literature and brief them on the programs we've developed. They get the staff and the teachers together, and share the information. Then they put it in a newsletter and send it to parents. We get participation and support from the parents, the

*Tasreen and Tariq celebrate her graduation
from the University of Washington.*

staff, the teachers. I'd love to see that kind of involvement in schools all over the country.

"Perhaps both the biggest asset and the biggest challenge for us is that everyone involved with the Foundation is here because they believe in its cause—but only Kit has been a professional nonprofit manager. The rest of us are figuring it out as we go, and what we lack in experience we try to make up with dedication and energy. So far it's working well. But at some point we'll probably have to have additional management resources on the team.

"The best part of what I'm doing is working with children. I love kids. Always have.

"The hardest part is that every day I'm reminded that my brother was murdered. Just answering the phone 'Tariq Khamisa Foundation' reminds me. The challenge for me is to stay emotionally strong enough to do the work without being torn apart over the loss of my brother. I want all the Foundation's work to be done well, for him.

"What I miss most about Tariq is just sitting out on the patio and talking for hours. We were such good friends. It's hard every time I realize I can't tell him what's going on in my life anymore. He was younger than I in age, but older and wiser in some ways. He gave me the most amazing advice. I miss the security of having a brother—someone I thought would be there for me all my life. Siblings have a special bond.

"I've only been at the Foundation a short time. But in terms of my career, right now I can't think of doing anything else."

Other People's Bardos

*I think of a bardo as being like a moment when you step
toward the edge of a precipice.*

Sogyal Rinpoche, *The Tibetan Book of Living and Dying*

Tariq's life was not likely to have touched the lives of
thousands of children. Through the Foundation's programs, his
death will. After our presentation at the Birney and Roosevelt
schools, we received many letters from the kids.

> *I'm glad that you came to my school. What you
> talked about is very important. What you said, I already
> knew but I'm glad you refreshed my memory. I am sorry
> to hear about Tony and Tariq, but I am very glad that
> somebody is doing something. I'm only in the sixth
> grade but I know from others' experiences what gangs,
> violence and drugs can do to people. I'm glad to know
> there are foundations like the TKF to help my future kids.*
>
> *Teresa*

> *I think it's important that you go to schools and tell
> kids they have a choice. The day you came to our
> school I was re-enlightened about what to do about peer
> pressure.*
> *I think it is wonderful that Tony's grandfather and
> Mr. Khamisa can work out their differences without
> using violence. I'm glad that they didn't stoop to using
> violence because my mother taught me when I was real
> young that two wrongs don't make a right.*

Some of the positive choices I will make are to stay in school, stay away from drugs, violence and crime, make my own decisions, and never give up.

Trisha

When you guys came to talk to us Birney kids I think you really made a difference in everybody. Even if it was a little one, sooner or later they're going to find out that they learned a lot. All the things you guys talk about I already knew but you guys really made me think about it. I'm glad people are getting together and trying to clean up this world—how God had it from the start.

Klarissa

You taught us some good points, like don't get yourself in bad places. I always try to make good choices. I know it is not fun getting in deep trouble, like when my brother broke into someone's house and stole. He had to stay in Juvenile Hall for eight days. I learned not to do that or the same thing can happen to me. When there is bad peer pressure I will stay away from it. The people I turn to for help is cops, friends, family and adults. The choices I will make for my whole life is not to do drugs, get in fights or get in trouble.

Unsigned

Thank you for coming and reminding me of peer pressure and gangs. I thought I might have to get in one but I think now I don't have to. There are lots of people I can turn to for help now but didn't know before. Talking about it helped me a lot. Seeing Tony in the courthouse pouring his feelings out, I thought I never want to be in that position ever. Now I am thinking about Tony. I knew Tony, we used to hang out together. Then he started to hang out with the gang. I was mad when he shot the pizza man over a pizza.

I wasn't really mad at Tony. I was mad at Q-Tip, the gang leader. I feel I am going to stay out of a gang, I'm not going to go down that road.

Unsigned

Well, when you guys came I thought it was going to be boring. But it really helped me a lot. It will help me make nonviolent choices when I am in peer pressure. I don't go to my parents because my parents aren't open to me. I've been thinking about my future and I want to go to college so I will not kill or hurt anybody. I want to be a good example for my children. I don't want them to kill somebody because of peer pressure.

Melissa

It made me think about a lot. Like peer pressure. Some of my friends try to pressure me into doing things I don't want to do. Now I know who I can turn to for help. I am going the make the right choice for my future. I will try not to use violence for anything.

Ebony

Sometimes, when I'm feeling blue and missing Tariq, reading these letters helps.

———

A child's directness and innocence can actually bring a sweetness, lightness, even sometimes a humor into the pain of dying.

Sogyal Rinpoche, *The Tibetan Book of Living and Dying*

———————

On April 17, 1997, I cut short some business in London to catch a British Airways flight to Washington, D.C. I was going to a ceremony of great personal importance: Ples and I had been selected for a National Crime Victim Award. The 16 recipients were chosen from over 200 nominations.

This recognition is given by the U.S. Justice Department to people whose work for victims' causes has had an impact. The program focuses heavily on those whose work may help avoid the creation of future victims.

I was looking forward to the event. I knew the other 14 award recipients would be going through their own bardos. For a brief period, we would find support and shared understanding with each other.

Also, I would be seeing René again: a young woman I had met at a victims' issues conference where I was the keynote speaker. She had lost a close friend to a vicious act of violence, and was working hard to overcome the loss.

In October 1994, just three months before I lost Tariq, horror entered René's life. Her best friend since childhood, a woman with the almost-identical name of Renee, had been brutally murdered after being abused by a drug addict and his girlfriend. They followed her home and forced their way into her apartment at gunpoint. She was 29 years old.

My new friend René decided she had to try to do something about violence in our communities. She quit her job, took a substantial pay cut, and went to work as an administrator for an organization called the Coalition of Juvenile Justice.

Clearly, we had some things in common.

On the flight I found myself wishing my family could attend, but they had been unable to make the long trip from the Pacific Northwest. I arrived at the hotel around 4:00 PM, took a short nap and a shower, and went to the orientation meeting. Ples had just gotten in from San Diego. We gave each other a big "hello" hug.

At the orientation, they briefed us on the plans for the following day. The award recipients would have lunch together after the ceremony. This would give us a chance to share our stories with each other. Then we would be taken to the White House. We were told there was a good chance President Clinton would have time to briefly meet with us. My heart skipped a beat: I, an immigrant from Kenya, might be shaking hands with the president of the United States!

Shortly after the Foundation began to attract media attention, I had sent President and Mrs. Clinton a letter. Part of it said, "... the war against the plight of children killing children is the most significant issue facing the nation today. And now, in the absence of an external enemy, we have to focus all our resources to fight the internal enemy—violence." I hoped I would get a chance to say this to the president in person.

After the orientation, I had dinner with René at a nearby Italian restaurant. I was foggy and jet-lagged, but the importance of what was going on filled me with energy.

———

At the ceremony the next morning, the award recipients were seated to the left of the podium, and officials from the Justice Department were on the right. The main auditorium in the Hall of Justice is a beautiful, majestic setting: a high, decorated ceiling, and huge doors probably built around the turn of the century. The setting and the charged atmosphere gave me goose bumps.

In addition to René, I had invited my friend Lou Adamo to attend the awards ceremony. Lou is executive director of an organization called RANCHO, dedicated to housing homeless farm workers. I had met Lou through my service as president of RANCHO's advisory board.

Just before the ceremony was to start, Lou, who had been studying the program package, said, "I see you're being specially honored. Only you and Ples have been selected to receive the Special Community Service Award." As I walked up to take my seat on the stage, I felt overcome by a storm of emotion: pride in our accomplishments; remembrance of Tariq; recognition of our family and the contributions of my community; and the power of the human spirit. The storm quickly calmed, and its components blended into a warm feeling of hope, peace, love and brother/sisterhood.

United States Attorney General Janet Reno has a reputation for punctuality, and she arrived precisely at 11 o'clock. The program began. Uniformed Marine Corps members presented the country's colors, and the singer provided a glorious rendition of the national anthem. Aileen Adams gave an introductory speech, then turned the microphone over to Janet Reno. Reno introduced each of us and spoke of our experiences. Each story touched me deeply.

Azim and Ples with Attorney General Janet Reno after receiving their Special Community Service Award from the Justice Department.

After her speech, Reno invited us to the podium one by one to receive our awards, and have our picture taken with her. Ples and I went up last. As we received our Special Community Service Award, Reno said, "These caretakers of a murder victim and of an offender recognized that their whole community was victimized by the violence that had shattered their lives. It took great courage for the two men to come together, as well as forgiveness and compassion."

As I took the plaque, Tariq was in my mind. An award like this helps give meaning to his life on earth, I thought.

Closing remarks from Aileen Adams ended the ceremony. She finished with a quote from an interview I had given *Parade* magazine, which they used to headline their story about the Foundation: "I realized change had to start with me." The program concluded with a song dedicated to all the award recipients: "You Are My Hero." As the singer sang ". . . you are the wind beneath my wings," I looked around. I felt I was, indeed, among heroes.

———

At the lunch, each of the award recipients talked of what had brought them here.

> **Ellen Halbert**: *Raped, beaten, stabbed, left for dead by a drifter. Left her job as a real estate broker to dedicate herself to victim services, and just finished a term as vice chair of the Texas Board of Criminal Justice.*

Sue Hathorn: *Motivated by the memory of an abused child that she saw returned to a home where he had been beaten, has waged a 20-year, one-woman campaign against child abuse in Mississippi.*

Janice Lienhart and **Sharon Nahorney**: *After their parents and aunt were brutally murdered by two teenagers, discovered there were no resources in Alaska that could help them deal with their grief, or with the justice system. Formed an organization to provide crucial victim services to homicide survivors.*

Pastor Roderick Mitchell: *As a child, on many a cold winter morning, had to flee the house with his mother and smaller siblings to hide in the cotton fields away from the reach of his abusive father. As an adult, opened his church to a rape crisis program in need of a home, then expanded the church's role to provide services to all victims of crime, particularly young people.*

Evelyn Dillon: *After her husband was murdered, founded a support coalition to provide outreach services to victims of violent crime. Has contributed 13,000 hours of volunteer assistance to people needing help.*

Viki Sharp: *Heads a "national model" program providing 24-hour, on-scene crisis intervention and emergency services. Eight members of her team provided services to Oklahoma City bombing victims.*

The program sponsors a teen team, specially trained as peer counselors. Both her daughters serve as youth counselors and advocates. Her nominator described her as a "masterful woman guided by her single-minded dedication to making a difference."

These were just some of the incredible tales of dedication and spirit I heard at that lunch. What an honor to be part of such a group! May the wind beneath their wings carry them far.

After lunch we were driven to the White House. Walking along the White House driveway on this windy, chilly day was awe-inspiring. To see this legendary edifice up close—the emblem of the glory and might of America—made me feel tiny, a pygmy confronted with grandeur.

Passing through what seemed like endless security procedures, we were shown into the Roosevelt conference room in the West Wing, next to the Oval Office. A White House staffer gave us the history of the artifacts in the room. My mind wandered over all the world leaders who had sat in this room, all the decisions that had been made . . .

After a 40-minute wait, Vice President Al Gore joined us, and assured us of his and the president's commitment to victims' rights. Each of us had the chance to speak and have our picture taken with him. President Clinton's schedule did not allow him to meet with us, but I was able to get a letter and package about the Foundation's work delivered to him and the First Lady.

We left the White House around 4 PM. The day had been powerful, unforgettable—and exhausting. René and I had a quiet dinner at the Two Quails restaurant, and I slowly felt myself unwinding. It was late when she dropped me off at the hotel.

Although I was tired, I lay in bed, aware and awake in a long meditation. I reflected on the events of the day, the people I had met, the myriad emotions I had felt. With a prayer for Tariq's soul to rest in eternal peace, I fell into a sound sleep.

Next morning, René dropped me off at the Union train station in Washington, D.C. I had two meetings scheduled in New York before returning to London to complete my business there.

On the train, I leaned back in my seat and closed my eyes. It was a good time to have a conversation with Tariq. We spoke often. He frequently encouraged me to live more, laugh more and work less. Tariq had loved life and laughed easily. I could learn a thing or two from him.

Strange, I thought. I had laughed a lot this weekend. I had shared some jokes with René. It felt good. It had been too long since I laughed.

The shifting and precarious nature of the bardo of becoming can also be the source of many opportunities for liberation.

Sogyal Rinpoche, *The Tibetan Book of Living and Dying*

Restorative Justice: A New Paradigm

The restorative justice model is based on the premise that crime occurs in the context of the community and the community must be involved in addressing it.

The Restorative Justice Project

I have said many times that my son's murder did not drive me toward "an eye for an eye." But make no mistake. Mine is not a wishy-washy, soft-on-crime, unfocused, bleeding-heart brand of compassion. It's a desire for true justice. And I have become absolutely convinced there's a better route to true justice than that provided by our traditional, punitive justice system.

Indeed, I am convinced that too often, our system provides no true justice at all.

You may have heard the saying, "Justice delayed is justice denied." It's an unfortunate fact of our current system that delay is business as usual. Proceedings are lengthy. In preparation for an adversarial/retributive trial, defense attorneys usually advise their clients not to admit anything. This can destroy any possibility that the offender might be inclined to do the right thing: take responsibility, express contrition, initiate a process of healing.

Victims file complaints, but otherwise they're relegated to the role of passive observer, not participant. They have little to say and less to do about the outcome of the eventual trial. And "eventual" may be too kind a word. Some cases seem tortuously open-ended, leaving everyone in total darkness and frustration. When will blessed resolution and closure arrive? No way to tell.

There's no immediacy, no sense of urgency.

Further, victims are likely to observe that there is a substantial amount of government infrastructure devoted to the offender. They see and read about defense *teams*, extensive rehab programs, treatment programs, inmates' rights suits, conjugal visit facilities, well-equipped prison gyms, probation programs, training programs—all financed by the public and all dedicated to the well-being of the criminal. Law-abiding citizens who have been victimized might well wonder why they're paying massive sums for a system that probably wouldn't even return their phone calls; for a system that views the criminal as its "client."

I saw one article in which victims were referred to as "props" in our system. In other words, the current system isn't working well for offenders, victims, or communities. We need a big-time priority shift.

We need justice. But what *is* justice? For many people, justice equals punishment. But to me, punishment alone seems hollow and incomplete. Whether the criminal we're talking about is a Midwest burglar I'll never meet, or the killer of my son, I believe we need more than just their punishment.

We need *restoration*. The wrongs done to us must be made right. The wrong things inside the criminal that led to this act must be made right—if possible. Only then can the criminal, too, be restored as a member of the community.

That's easy to say; it's damn hard to do. In some cases it's impossible to do. Property can be replaced. Some bodily injuries can heal and pass. But serious injury might never heal. And death is final. How can a life be restored once it's ended?

It can't, of course. Yet there *is* a form of restoration we can have even after the loss of a loved one's life. I want to tell you about an inspiring, relatively new approach to dealing with criminals and crime. Then I'll explain how this new paradigm would work for me personally, and bring me as much restoration after the death of my son as I could hope to have.

The approach is called *restorative justice* (I'll abbreviate it as "RJ"). To keep the focus on events I have experienced, in this chapter I am only talking about RJ as it applies to dealing with *youthful* offenders. I do support a form of it for adult offenders as well, but it is more complicated when dealing with adults.

In the context of juvenile criminals, I can say clearly and without hesitation: *I want to see our system changed to a restorative justice approach.*

An eye for an eye makes the whole world blind.

Mohandas Gandhi

RJ's most dramatic departure from the traditional criminal justice system (which is sometimes called a "retributive justice" system, since it focuses on retribution and punishment) revolves around the role of government. In the traditional model, a crime is not considered primarily an offense against the victim and the community. It is an offense against *government* and *government laws.* Damage to the victim and damage to the community are shunted to the background. In fact, you often hear defense attorneys saying things like, "My client doesn't owe anything to the victim. What happens now is just between him and the state." That's factually true under our current system. But that truth carries deep problems.

By defining their obligation only in relation to the government, we provide no incentive for criminals to fix what they have broken. When they finish prison sentences, we often say they have "paid their debt to society." Excuse me? What, exactly, have they "paid"? And who is the "society" they've paid it to? Serving time behind bars is not "paying"—at least not in the sense of returning something taken and owed. And the government, in this situation, is not a usable surrogate for society.

But the phrase "paying their debt to society" does contain a vital concept. That's what *should* happen. The challenge is to *correctly* define "payment" and "society," then provide a structure through which the right payment is made to the right people. Offenders must be held accountable, and responsible to make things right with the victims and communities they harm.

The offender has created a problem. The offender should help solve it.

And if the community simply turns its problems over to "the system" for others to solve, it ceases to be a real community. The "system" can't *motivate* offenders to want to live an upstanding life. (Scaring them is not a long-term solution.) But a community can. The "system" can't comfort and support victims. A community can.

You might ask, "Why should we care what happens to criminals? After all, they're *criminals*. All they deserve is punishment." I believe there are three very good reasons we should care.

First, the vast majority of criminals do return to society at some point. In California, the only crime which carries a death sentence or life in prison without possibility of parole is first-degree murder with special circumstances. Most other criminals are going to rejoin the community. If they can't heal and be restored as functioning members of it, there's a good chance they'll return to crime. When that happens, they lose, their new victims lose, we all lose.

We must find a way to bring them in. When people feel connected to a group, they're much less likely to harm its members.

Second, I believe that every human is the repository of unique gifts. With few exceptions, despite criminals' bad acts, *something* of value is buried within them. As with the mining of precious metals, it might require a lot of effort to find it, dig it out, get it to the surface, separate it from the dross, polish it and reveal its value. But each of us has something to offer that's ours alone, not duplicated in anyone else. The more we mine all our resources and allow them to contribute to the community, the richer our lives will be.

I will never be comfortable with the idea of slamming doors shut forever. I can never be comfortable cutting myself off from the chance that people might have something rare and valuable to give me—even if they once made a terrible mistake.

Third, and perhaps most important: the victim needs to heal, too. When we are victimized by a criminal act, it is natural to feel anger. But permanent, unabated anger is destructive to us. It fills us with tension and hatred. It can become a consuming fire that blocks out love and joy. We feel that the anger is aimed at someone else: that criminal who harmed us. But left unchecked, the anger harms *us*.

We've all read stories about criminals who have come to terms with the wrong they have done, and want to find a way to atone. Often, one of the first things they do is ask for forgiveness from the victim of their crime. That need for forgiveness is a vital part of our human makeup. When we know we've done bad things to others, that becomes a festering wound on our insides. To cleanse and heal that wound, we need absolution from those we've hurt.

The criminal needs the victim's forgiveness to heal. And in one of human nature's strange twists, full healing for the victim may require him or her to grant that forgiveness. There may be no other way to put down the destructive anger.

On the other hand, no one wants to feel used. No one wants to be a sucker. Forgiveness is not going to be casually handed out as if it were penny candy. The stage must be properly set. That's what RJ tries to do.

———————

Ron Claassen is co-director of the Center for Peacemaking and Conflict Studies at Fresno Pacific College. His article, "Restorative Justice—Fundamental Principles," provides an excellent summary of what's involved in crafting an RJ system. Here are his main points:

Crime is primarily an offense against human relationships, and *secondarily* a violation of law. In other words, we need to skip the middleman, and focus on who's really involved.

Restorative justice recognizes that after crime occurs, there is danger and opportunity. The danger is that the community, the victim and the offender all emerge from the experience feeling alienated and damaged. The opportunity is to manage resolution so all participants are restored, and feel they belong to a society which is functional and worthwhile. Under the retributive model, the outcome is rarely more than jail time following a conviction. Underlying causes of the crime are not addressed, and neither is healing of the victim.

Restorative justice focuses on making things as right as possible. Ideally, the offender can and will contribute to fixing the property and emotional damage he or she has caused. If offenders can be persuaded to take that responsibility, beneficial things can happen: for the offender, for the victim, for the community. We all know how powerful an apology can be. Restorative justice encourages an apology of both words and deeds.

Restorative justice views the situation as a teachable moment for the offender. It is a time for educational effort. The offender must be shown the damage suffered by a victim who is real, not faceless. Effort must be made to address the breakdown in the offender's value system that resulted in harming this victim and the whole community.

Restorative justice proposes a cooperative response structure that involves all the affected parties, not just government representatives. This might include the victim and the victim's family, the offender and the offender's family, community representatives, clergy, witnesses, as well as officials. The goal is to get the wisdom of many voices and viewpoints in planning the path to restoration.

Once agreements, decisions or commitments are made, restorative justice recognizes the need for follow-up and accountability, and the "natural community" should be used as much as possible. This is an important "reality check," because there's a risk here. Offenders who conclude a restorative justice process with an agreement to do things which will repair and heal the damage they've caused had better do it. Failure at this stage might leave the victim feeling violated a second time. In light of this risk . . .

Restorative justice recognizes that not all offenders will choose to be cooperative. Even the most ardent RJ proponent doesn't want to be a naïve or careless enabler of further damage to the community. Some offenders may be unwilling to participate in a restoration process for themselves or their victims. In the interests of community safety, the retributive justice model may have to be used in those cases. However, the opportunity for restoration should always be kept open and encouraged. Even retributive treatment should include teaching tools and skills which give offenders a chance at eventual success—and the values and ethics that invite them to aspire to success.

One specific program which implements the RJ approach is known as a "Victim-Offender Reconciliation Program." VORPs have been established in communities in the U.S. and some European countries. The key to this program is the use of trained volunteer mediators from the community. These mediators meet separately with the victim and the offender. They explain the program. They find out what happened, why it happened, and what each party's issues and feelings are. They invite participation in the program.

If they agree to the program, the victim and the offender are brought together to negotiate restitution: what can the offender do to make amends to the victim? What will the victim require to feel repaired, to accept the offender as a member of the community again? Both parties tell the other their feelings and concerns about the offense. They talk *directly to each other*, not via third-party interrogation in a courtroom. The volunteer facilitates the meeting. If it is successfully concluded, a written agreement is signed specifying what the offender will do.

I'm sure you can imagine how difficult it is for both parties when victim and offender sit down together. Getting all that anger and defensiveness out of the way is a tough battle. It's not our nature to easily let go of deeply held feelings. There's work involved. To make it happen, both parties have to want it.

VORP administration may include enforcement of the agreement, such as collecting and transmitting agreed-upon payments to the victim. It may also include services to help offenders find the jobs they need to earn the payments. Think how much more constructive this is than their languishing on a cot in a cell.

Through this reconciliation process, anger and alienation on both sides can be overcome. The victim wins. The offender wins. The *community* wins. A publication from the Victim-Offender Reconciliation Program of the Central Valley, in California, says:

> *VORP helps offenders face the real human and*
> *financial costs of their actions. It helps them ask*
> *forgiveness by recognizing the victim's feelings,*

accepting responsibility to make restitution, and
clarifying intentions for the future. Offenders have a
direct part in setting restitution, resulting in ownership
for the decision and for its fulfillment. VORP gives the
offender a chance to become a productive rather than a
dependent member of the community. It helps stop the
cycle of crime for many offenders.

In an article entitled "Restoring Justice," Joanne Cvar references results from a Victim-Offender Reconciliation Program in Oregon:

> *Ninety percent of participants fulfill their restitution*
> *agreements, and only 6 percent of program participants*
> *under age 17 who have completed the program get into*
> *further trouble with the law. In contrast, the recidivism*
> *rate for government-run juvenile correction programs is*
> *about 96 percent, according to the* Oregonian
> *newspaper.*

An additional word that has entered the restorative justice vocabulary is "balanced." The word provides a valuable reminder to us that in considering this new paradigm, we must not lose sight of the fact that each interest involved must be given equal importance. It would be easy to regard the criminal's restorative obligations as another form of retribution. (In fact, in his article "The Campaign for Equity-Restorative Justice," John Wilmerding points out that there can be a "backslide . . . into the emotionally based, vindictive idea represented by the quintessentially retributive slogan, 'It's payback time!'")

On the other side, it would be equally easy to focus just on the issues involving the offender. But ultimately, we must never forget that RJ must be seen as helpful and right for both victim *and* offender. Without widespread victim support, the concept will be doomed to very limited usage. Making things right for victims requires offenders to be truly remorseful for what they have done. When we're trying to figure out if RJ can be successfully applied in a specific case, that's a giant variable in the equation.

In an article called "Putting Victims First" in *State Government News,* victims' advocate Anne Seymour says, "Victims should be at the forefront of restorative justice practices, not an afterthought. Victims are often left out, as was admitted at a recent symposium. There, a community practitioner said, 'We don't always invite victims to the table of restorative justice.' My answer was that if victims aren't invited to the table, you can't serve supper."

And neither victim nor offender perspectives must be permitted to drown out the community's need for safety and a functional society.

So, "balance" reminds us to include everyone in this justice model. In their article, "Balanced and Restorative Justice," Gordon Bazemore and Mark Umbreit identify three dynamics as the cornerstones on which that balance is built:

Accountability. When a crime occurs, a debt incurs. Justice requires that every effort be made by offenders to restore losses suffered by victims.

Competency development. Offenders should leave the juvenile justice system more capable of productive participation in conventional society than when they entered.

Community protection. The public has a right to a safe and secure community; juvenile justice should develop a progressive response system to ensure offender control in the community.

———

Another conceptual framework which incorporates RJ in its model has been called *community justice*. This concept emphasizes the importance of the community having the power to participate in responding to crime in its midst. It links restorative justice with proactive, crime-preventing community policing.

Community policing elevates the concept of what a police force should do. It goes beyond the role of uniforms responding to 911 calls; beyond just "the cops." It's reminiscent of an earlier era, before we got so big and complicated.

Maybe it descends from the patrolman on his beat. He lived in the neighborhood. He walked around all day. Everyone knew him, and he knew everyone. He gave the time of day to people without watches, and directions to people without maps. He advised mischievous teens—and sometimes pulled them out of trouble and hauled them home. He rescued cats, helped the elderly cross the street, knew who was on vacation and kept an eye on their houses. When necessary, he got the citizenry involved in upholding law and order.

He didn't just respond to problems. By being there—a visible, intrinsic part of a community's upstanding values—he helped *prevent* problems. It wasn't that he was the community's pillar; he was a symbol that the community *had* a pillar. The pillar was the community members themselves: their values, their involvement with each other's welfare.

One article I read on the community justice system pointed out that the *return on investment* in a community justice system can be very high: increased safety, security and fairness. As a businessman, I respond to "return on investment." And what we've been getting from our retributive justice system, as it relates to youth, is a negative return with a high recidivism rate (insult added to injury).

Restorative justice is being tried in a few places, and I hope we'll see more of it. I know about programs in Vermont, Minnesota, Oregon and California, and there are others. Every time I hear that it's being used it gladdens my heart, because I know it can work wonders.

Perpetrators have had their lives turned around. Victims have been healed because they have been able to articulate and explain their devastation. Perpetrators usually don't understand the damage they do until they hear it from the victim's perspective.

I read a story about two teenagers in Minnesota who burgled someone's house. When they were caught, the victim told the judge he didn't want to send them to jail. He wanted to meet with them and get them to do something good for the community. Eventually, it was agreed that the two teenagers would prepare the food for a neighborhood picnic, and serve it to the neighbors. At the picnic, they heard how their crime had affected the people who live there. The story said the victim was satisfied with the outcome, the community sounded satisfied (and stuffed!), and the teenagers have not gotten into any further trouble.

Another situation involved an Oregon teenager who had been a repeat shoplifter at a local store. He finally got caught. Under traditional, retributive justice, it would have been off to jail or a juvenile detention facility for him. In that setting, he might have learned things we really don't want a teenager to know. He might have found himself in a group which encouraged him to commit more serious crimes when he got out.

But the manager of the store agreed to let him make restoration by working at the store without pay. He did good work. In fact, he did such good work that the manager ended up giving him a permanent job there.

Are these major triumphs? No. Is the seriousness of these crimes anywhere near what Tony did to Tariq? Of course not. Do these anecdotal accounts really *prove* anything? I can't say for sure that they prove anything. But they show us some possibilities. And they give us some hope.

I saw a great quote on RJ from a member of the U.S. House of Representatives. It was in an article called "Righting Wrongs," by Michael Scott, in *State Government News*. Florida representative Wesley Skoglund, chair of the House Judiciary Committee, doesn't agree with the arguments that RJ is "soft on crime."

"I argue that sitting on a cot watching cartoons is soft on crime," he says. "People like the idea of putting offenders to work. When I ask, 'Wouldn't you rather see them shoveling snow in January?' people say 'Yes!' They love it!"

Does this mean we let *violent* criminals work off the harm they have wrought by just shoveling snow? Absolutely not. It is true that restorative justice works best when offenders get back into the community as soon as possible. But community safety and security is a paramount concern. No violent offender can be permitted to threaten peaceful people. Violent offenders have to be separated from the community until they no longer represent a threat.

But we need to use that separation time productively. There are restorative contributions inmates can make to the community even when they're confined. They should be guided down that path. "Victim empathy" programs can show them the damage they've done. Vocational training can teach them how to do productive work and earn a living. (Computer technology gives us a new field with enormous potential.) Counseling and treatment programs should be offered to give offenders a chance to learn how to manage and control violent behavior. If they're able to learn that—*truly* learn it, not just learn it enough to fool an evaluator—then they should be given the chance for eventual restoration.

Some will learn quickly. Some will take longer. Sadly, some will never learn.

————————

Adam's children are the limbs of one another
For in creation, they are from one substance.

When time causes pain to one limb
The other limbs cannot rest in peace.

If you do not care for others' affliction
You do not deserve to be called human.

Sadi, 13th century Persian Sufi poet

————————

There's lots of work ahead to figure out how RJ and traditional, retributive justice should fit together. Some of the theory needs to be fleshed out with concrete, practical approaches. Some of the practical details need better theoretical support. But it's moving forward.

The simplest administrative approach is when an offender can plead guilty, receive a suspended retributive sentence, and agree to meet with a reparations board or a victim-offender mediator. Upon successful completion of the restorative agreement, the suspended retributive sentence is discharged as well.

Two of the big challenges currently facing RJ are nailing down when it can be successfully substituted for retributive justice, and consistently tailoring the correct restorative sentence to fit the crime. These areas are likely to remain more art than science until we get more data and experience with the RJ approach.

An important fact to keep in mind is that when restorative justice can be made to work, traditional justice resources are freed up to focus on the most serious crimes and criminals. I think we can all agree that if we don't *have* to have more prisons, there are more attractive things to do with our tax dollars.

———

America has always had the "frontier spirit," so things change faster here than anywhere else. But our society is large, diverse, complex. Restorative justice is not going to replace a well-entrenched retributive justice system overnight, or even over a few years. If it happens, it will happen gradually. Ongoing change will need to be fueled by frequent success stories.

Dennis Maloney is in the front line of people trying to expand the use of restorative justice. He's been a corrections professional for 27 years, and is currently Director of Community Justice for Deschutes County in Oregon.

"As I worked my way through corrections jobs," Maloney recalls, "I got involved in programs that focused on holding offenders accountable for what they had done to victims—rather than just holding them accountable to the institution of government. I started seeing a much deeper appreciation on behalf of the offenders for the human consequences of their crimes. Instead of just dealing with courts and probation officers, offenders had to deal with real people they had hurt.

"I ended up writing a book challenging the traditional premise of the justice system, and calling for a more *balanced* approach between the interests of victims and those of offenders. We have focused too much on offenders. The focus of criminal justice is, 'Who done it, and what are we going to do to them?' The focus of restorative justice is to look at crime as a wound which must be healed. RJ elevates the place of victims in the system.

"In a sense, you might say victims become the 'customer' of the system. Now, it's almost as if offenders are the customer. Under RJ, offenders must re-earn 'customer' status by helping to heal the peace of the communities which they have shattered by their acts. And in helping communities and victims heal, perhaps offenders can help their own healing.

"When violence is involved, mediation can be very difficult and sensitive. It can take a year to prepare for a victim to meet a perpetrator. But because it can be so therapeutic, the effort spent in making this happen correctly can be worth all the work.

"Sometimes what the victim needs is an answer to the most basic question: 'Why? Why did you do this to me?' Or, 'Why did you do this to my loved one?' And the next thing they need to hear is genuine remorse and contrition for the act. Often what they want the offender to do, as part of the restoration process, is commit to telling *other* people, perhaps lesser offenders, why they shouldn't do what this perpetrator did. They want the offender to try to get others to promise never to hurt someone else. When victims feel they may have helped save others from their terrible experience, somehow it seems to empower them and make them feel they've contributed something important to the community.

"Under the traditional system, almost all justice-related government services are designed for the offender. We need to balance that out, and also provide services to victims. Perhaps effective, therapeutic counseling is a good place to start—giving them the tools to piece their lives back together. We have a whole bunch of psychologists and psychiatrists who work with offenders, but we've never thought about fielding a team like that for victims.

"There's a very effective program in California called "Mothers of Murdered Children." These mothers actually travel to the state's correctional institutions and tell their stories to large groups of juvenile offenders who have not yet committed crimes of violence. Victims *need* to tell their story. Bringing out their words of grief and loss helps them. Having someone *really listen* to victims' stories is an important part of the restorative justice model.

"There are those who might see RJ as 'soft on criminals,' and they could be tough to sell on the concept. I'm a parent of five children, and I can understand the emotions that surge up when a child is hurt. But if you look at the lives of those who get locked into lifelong hatred and anger—they never heal! There's no hope for healing. And the trauma of continuous hate and anger hits them with yet another form of stress, in addition to the effect the original crime had on them.

"I remember when Azim told me that as long as he stayed in a state of anger and hate, he impeded the development of his son's afterlife. That was a unique cultural and spiritual perspective to me. But he was one of the first victims of violence I ever heard take a look at what had happened outside the framework of hatred and anger. And what I witnessed in his life was, even though he was still in a process of mourning, he started to show signs of getting healthy again. He started to heal.

"When he got in contact with Tony's family, and started the Foundation's program to help all America deal with youth violence, you could see him go from a person who had nothing but tragedy in his eyes, to a person who had some spark return to his eyes.

"I've dealt with folks who have not been able to get there yet. They still have that anger in their eyes, and it's not healthy. And yet, it's so easy to see why they're in that place, given the loss they've suffered. But I would hope that as they came in contact with people like Azim, they would see a way healing can begin—and see that there can be hope for people who have lost family members to violent crime. I can't help but feel that if they can't get past the anger and the hate, there's no hope for them.

"My prognosis for increased acceptance and use of RJ is very strong. In the traditional criminal justice system, nobody wins. Victims lose because they don't get to play a meaningful enough role in the process, and they get no restitution. Offenders lose because they get a punitive sentence that doesn't let them try to right their wrong, removes them from society, and doesn't prepare them for restoration to the community. Also, it almost guarantees that they'll never really *feel* the impact their behavior had on the victim, and they'll never experience any empathy. All of the above causes high recidivism rates. So we have to keep building more prisons. That takes money away from everything, from education to victims' services.

"Getting offenders to feel empathy for others in the community is important. When people really feel that, they won't steal from someone else, and they sure won't hurt them. And nothing in the criminal justice system stimulates empathy.

"Under RJ, the person who figures most prominently is the person who suffered the loss. What could be more just? Surveys show very high victim satisfaction with the results of RJ, and very low satisfaction with the results of criminal justice.

"It's also a fact that when offenders commit to pay restitution under an RJ agreement, they are far more likely to actually carry out that commitment than they are in the rare case when there is court-ordered restitution.

"One of the debilitating effects of being a crime victim is the feeling of powerlessness. Being part of the RJ process, and having a say in what the offender has to do to earn redemption— earn a way back into the community—helps restore the victim's feeling of normal empowerment.

"Offenders doing restorative work can have a powerful community-building effect. In our community, offenders are helping us build a Habitat For Humanity house from scratch. They've helped us build a homeless shelter. They've helped build a child abuse treatment center. They've worked on creating parks. So the message we've sent to the offender is, 'You made a mistake. You're not going to be *granted* forgiveness, but you can *earn* forgiveness through serving the community and restoring the peace.'

"The biggest impediment to RJ is some of our American cultural characteristics. I call it 'the American urge.' We're cool to victims. We're quick to banish offenders. And we favor institution-based solutions rather than relationship-based solutions. But we're more willing to consider RJ for juvenile offenders than adults, because we figure they have more chance of turning themselves around.

"If you look at other cultures' traditions, you see that frequently they structure justice through a restorative arrangement between offender and victim, with a community member or elder facilitating the settlement. Our notions of justice were largely imported from England, and their approach harks back to the days of William the Conqueror. He reasoned that as king, he owned the land and the people. Therefore, all crimes were crimes against him—the state. So he set up the system of fines payable to his treasury, and of having the king's attorney as a 'prosecutor' representing his interests. If you committed a crime, you were accountable to the king. Victims got lost. Compensation to the king for crimes committed became the only issue.

"When we adopted the English Code of Common Law, which included this philosophy of criminal justice, we installed a system which I believe is based on a faulty premise. We have now lived 200 years under that premise, and it's not going to be easy to overcome.

"It's also true that there's a lot of vested interest in the current system. I think some members of our judiciary like being treated as kings! Under a community-based mediation process, lawyers and judges and officers of the court would play a reduced role. They may see this as a threat, and be resistant to change.

"But if victims continue to have a favorable experience with restorative justice, it will happen."

———————

As you've read this chapter, I'm sure it's occurred to you that an RJ approach for a kid caught stealing a Snickers bar from a grocery store—or even heisting an unoccupied car—is light years easier than figuring out how to apply RJ to a killer. And it is. So how does it apply in our case?

Tariq is dead. My family and I are the living victims of the crime which took his life. The RJ concept requires us to be restored, made whole. That is the killer's responsibility. But obviously, Tony can't bring Tariq back. Murder, the obliteration of life, is a crime which might drown the possibility of restoration in a dark sea of never-ending loss. So how could he restore us?

The answer is: through my spiritual beliefs. Those beliefs are my buoy in that sea. They will not let me drown. They will not let me feel comfort or righteousness in writing off Tony Hicks. They remind me there is a soul in Tony that might still offer us good things. He got off to a terrible start. But his story is not yet over.

When I reached out to Ples, he was quick to take my hand. He made it clear he would do whatever he could to help with the work of the Foundation. In that moment, his spirit met mine. In that moment, a flash of restoration happened.

Later, Ples promised that he would stay my friend and be part of my emotional support system, helping me deal with the loss of my son, for the rest of his life. When he told me he promised Tony he would do that, I felt another touch of restoration.

I believe it was largely the outreach, the bond, the friendship that developed between Ples and me, that made Tony decide to plead guilty; to be held accountable; to not put me and my family—and his—through the agony of a trial. Truthfully, I don't know how I could have gotten through a trial.

It is my belief that Tony has crossed the initial hurdles for his restoration: he has accepted responsibility; he feels remorse; he has asked for my forgiveness. Yes, he will serve a retributive jail term. It will be longer than I would like. He has been sentenced under the laws of our state.

Despite those laws, there is nothing the State of California can do to help my restoration. But Tony can. If he dedicates himself to finding ways to combat youth violence, he will. If he helps me make my son's name a force for good, he will. And by accepting responsibility and expressing true remorse, he allowed me to start my own healing.

I am filled with the hope that eventually my restoration and Tony's will walk side by side in partnership.

In the meantime, something a woman said to me at a restorative justice conference last year still rings in my mind. I had given a speech at the conference. Afterward, she came up to me and said, "My husband was killed by a teenager 18 months ago. I have had more healing and more understanding of restorative justice in this last hour and a half than I had in the last 18 months. You have touched me."

And she has touched me back. Helping her heal helps me heal.

This transformation in criminal justice is not just one more new program in a 200-year succession of failed programs, but a revolution in the paradigm—a change of heart, as well as a change of mind.

Joanne Lucas Cvar, "Restoring Justice,"
in *Context* magazine, no. 36

Forgiveness

Out beyond ideas of wrongdoing and rightdoing,
there is a field. I'll meet you there.

Jelaluddin Rumi, *Quatrain 158*

When does a bardo end?

When can we say we're no longer in a transitional state? Is there a cosmic exit sign off the "bardo freeway"? Or a marker saying, "End of bardo, two months ahead"?

Permanent mysteries are woven into the fabric of our lives. That's frustrating, but necessary. Some things we couldn't bear to know.

It has been over three years since I lost Tariq, but we stay in touch. I have dinner with him often. I put his picture on the table facing me and tell him what's going on, what I've been thinking, what's new with the family. Nothing he doesn't already know, probably, but I like to tell him anyway.

———

Wednesday, January 21, 1998: The three-year anniversary of Tariq's death. I was in London on a business trip. I knew this day would be tough, and I had scheduled no meetings.

I spent Tuesday night with my friend Alan. I met Alan when I was 15 and attending school in London. I think he's now about

60, but I'm not entirely sure because over the years he has continually lied about his age. I knew I'd feel safe and supported at his house, as the inevitable painful memories gathered themselves for their anniversary visit.

Wednesday was spent with Nizar, my uncle, friend, business partner. I wanted to go to the mosque with him and his wife. They gathered the ingredients for me to cook a special meal at their house: kuku-paka, a dish of chicken in coconut milk. Tariq liked kuku-paka, and I had often made it for him.

I took the kuku-paka to the prayer hall. Part of the Ismaili tradition is to auction off the dishes brought by the community after the prayer service is over. It's a form of sharing with each other, and it's our belief that the satisfaction of the appetite reaches the departed soul.

That Wednesday had additional significance. It was Lailat al-Quadr, the anniversary of the day the Prophet Mohammed received his first revelation. Prayers are conducted all through this special night, and we believe they have the benefit of 1,000 nights of prayer. I stayed at the mosque until 1:00 AM.

The community and the sacred evening got me through January 21 in better shape than I expected. Thursday, the 22nd, it was back to work, meetings . . . and emotional dismay. The prior day had been the anniversary of Tariq's death. This day was the anniversary of my finding out about it. Emptiness hit me that day, hit me hard. The void was back. I was in my business meetings in body, but not in mind or soul. Raw pain felt like it was wiping out much of the healing which had slowly taken place over the last three years.

The pain wasn't just mental or emotional. It was physical as well. My body hurt, physically, with the need to rumple his hair, give him a bear hug, put an arm around his shoulder—just touch my son.

Somehow I got through the day, and stayed up late that night with friends. They kept reminding me of the work the Foundation was doing. It helped. I finally got to bed for three hours of bad sleep.

The next morning I left for Seattle. On the plane I read the poetry of the Sufi master, Rumi. Tasreen met me at the airport, and we drove to Vancouver with Almas for the special three-year prayers to be held for Tariq on Saturday.

Before the ceremony I visited Tariq's grave, as I do each time I go to Vancouver. I brought flowers and incense, put them on the grave, and said silent prayers. Then I walked slowly around the cemetery for an hour and a half, seeking inner shelter, my exhaled breath forming white frost puffs in the cool Canadian air.

A lot of work goes into preparation for the three-year prayer ceremony. Cooked dishes, fruit, chocolate, jewelry, clothing and other items are brought to Jamatkhana (the prayer hall) for the benefit of the departed, and for later auction. Being with my family and in sacred surroundings salved the soreness in my soul.

We left the mosque at 8:30 PM and had dinner at Almas' mother's house. At 10:30 we were on the road back to Seattle. We got in around 1:00 AM.

I had gotten almost no sleep for three nights, and it was going to get worse before it got better. Tasreen was moving to San Diego to go to work at her brother's Foundation, and I had business issues waiting for me there. Sunday morning we got up at 7:00 AM, loaded stuff into a rented U-Haul trailer, and took off. We drove all day and night—25 hours straight, stopping only for meals and caffeine infusions. As we approached the end of the drive, I was suffering less from emotional funk than from sleep deprivation.

By the time we got to my townhouse Monday morning, I was practically delirious. I felt as I had in Bulgaria shortly after Tariq's death, when I hadn't been able to sleep and had tried to walk myself into exhaustion. Lack of sleep does such strange things to the mind. That night, I took a sleeping pill—the first I had needed for a long time.

———————

The three-year anniversary, and the accompanying prayer ceremony in Vancouver, put me in a deeply reflective, philosophical mood. I wanted to probe the recesses of my spirit. Even my closest Ismaili friends had told me that although they would not have harbored hate if a loved one had been killed, they could not have stretched out the hand of peace. What was the *real* reason I had taken my path?

Somehow, the loss of Tariq hurled me back to my source. It took me to a place I had never consciously visited. It brought me *connection* with my soul and my higher being. It brought me into the loving arms of my Maker, my Divinity, and He sent me back with something I needed.

If I could write a letter to my son, this is what I would say:

Dear Tariq,

Thank you for the many gifts that have come my way as a result of your tragic loss. I have realized in the aftermath of the third anniversary of your death just how much these gifts have contributed to my spiritual journey.

With all my love,
Dad

I'm a down-to-earth investment banker, not a mystic. I don't want to sound like I have routine, two-way conversations with God, although I'd love to. I'm sure we all would. But I pray and meditate, and there are times when I experience a midprayer or midmeditation "high": the balm of soothing, wise energy; a refreshing swim in the river of knowledge and compassion. At a key point, when I needed it most, I emerged from one of those dips with the gift of enough grace to keep me afloat.

No conversations. But God is my *silent partner*, the unseen hand that directs me and the Foundation. We could not otherwise have made the progress we have. As Tasreen pointed out, none of us has done anything like this before.

If someone had come to me two and a half years ago and asked for my professional advice about starting a business with no product, no money and no experience, I would have said, "That's crazy!" Yet that's just what we did. Somehow, we had been made ready to do it.

During its early days, the Foundation seemed God-sent in another sense: it gave the family a way to talk about Tariq in the context of hopeful, forward-looking, positive activities . . . not just grief, loss and the past.

––––––––––

The ways Tariq's life would have changed or influenced mine are impossible to tell. His death may have changed me more than his life ever would have. Is that sad? Or mystically meaningful? I don't know yet.

What I do know is that his death has taken me down roads I would never have traveled. Before losing him, if I had been asked to name my top life priority, the answer would probably have been "international investment banking." And although ethical conduct and spirituality have always been part of my personal mission statement, if someone had asked what my single most important goal was, it might have been *"to be the best* international investment banker."

Now, winds of change have howled through my life, snatching pieces up, whirling them around, tossing them back shaken and dislocated. Everything is in post-apocalyptic flux and must be re-examined. Prior assumptions no longer apply. The world may not need another international investment banker, compared to other things it needs, as much as I thought it did.

Yes, I still make my living as a financial consultant. I enjoy it, and I'm proud of the service and value I provide my clients. But that work no longer occupies the top spot in my life's priorities. That spot is reserved for the fight to stop youth violence, and the work of the Tariq Khamisa Foundation.

I will go anywhere, I will do anything, anytime, if it will help win the struggle. I'll give speeches, talk to kids, support schools, meet with government officials, give interviews. I'll pass up no opportunity to move this cause forward. That is *the* priority.

When I first started giving speeches to groups, the pain of talking about Tariq's death could be overwhelming. Sometimes, before a speech, I would turn to Dan Pearson and say, almost pleadingly, "Do I have to go up there and tell the story again?" Dan would ask, "Do you want to save children's lives?" And I'd say, "Yes. I guess I answered my own question." And I had, because that is *the* priority.

I have been told that with my professional hat on, I was usually a hard-driving, hard-nosed guy who could also be a real S.O.B. After Tariq's death, Dan Pearson remembers my brother Nazir saying, "I think that facing his own demons has made Azim kinder, gentler, more thoughtful." Dan tells me that the loss of my son has tempered and humbled me.

What stubborn clay we humans are. Why does it take such dire events to get us to clean up our acts?

———————

I look back on the emotional roller coaster of the last three years, and marvel at the strength and resilience of the human psyche. Three years ago, a blinding moment of tragedy crushed me, emptied me of joy, filled me with despair. Any vision of a fulfilling life was destroyed. Now, paradoxically, it is through responding to that tragedy that I have found the road back to fulfillment.

The return from death to life was not smooth or consistent. It was one step forward, one back; three forward, two back; four forward, six back. There were days of spring bloom and days of winter thunder. At times I felt certain I would pull through; other times I was so mired in grief and longing for what might have been that survival seemed impossible.

Survival brought me face to face with another paradox: through death, I learned the glory and beauty of life. I also learned that each life reflects beauty in its own way. Each life destroyed is an irrevocable loss. Once gone, no amount of money or human power can recoup that loss.

How can we take life for granted? I never will again. I implore you not to.

I also implore you to appreciate your family every day. How easy to take those familiar faces for granted! Without my family I could not have survived. They were there at every moment of need—constant sources of strength and support, encouragement and counsel, love and prayer. At each step of my path, each step of the Foundation's creation, I relied on the combined wisdom of the family. We are one, joined in common purpose. There will be no such thing as *my* success, only *our* success.

———————

Winds of change stormed through Ples Felix's life with the same irresistible force they unleashed on mine. Comrade-in-arms, fellow crusader, new friend: my relationship with Ples is truly an example of a wonderful harvest rising miraculously from a bloody battlefield.

Ples is part of my restoration. I enjoy recalling a piece of banter that developed during one of our early conversations. He had commented on some problems facing African-Americans in this country. There are many such problems, of course, but I didn't necessarily agree with his perspective in this case. So I finally told him, "Ples, you shouldn't even be calling yourself an African-American. You were born here. You're an American through and through. You're an American-African, not an African-American. But I was born in Africa. I immigrated to the U.S. *I'm the African-American here, Ples, not you!*" And we shared a fine chuckle.

Peter Deddeh had a powerful insight about Ples, and the challenge he faces compared to mine. "One never gets over the death of a son," Peter said. "That memory will always be there for Azim, always painful. He's without Tariq. He's had to deal with that situation, live with it, find a way to move on.

"But Ples' situation, in a way, is more complicated. It will be continually evolving. How Tony is doing in CYA, how he's doing when he gets transferred to state prison, what happens to him over time—all this may actually put Ples through a wider *range* of emotions than Azim.

"There will be times when Tony's doing well, times when he's doing badly. There will be times when Tony and Ples may be estranged, times when Ples feels like giving up. Sometimes the system may make it impossible for Ples to do things for Tony that he thinks Tony needs. For the next 20-plus years, there will be a whole host of problems Ples will have to face that Azim actually won't. In a way, the *finality* of the fate of Azim's son allows him, perhaps, to refocus his life more easily than Ples can."

Ples said I can count on him being there for me. So shall I be there for him. We were joined by fate. Joined in friendship we shall stay.

After Tariq's death, I had to journey through a pair of crossroads. One required me to choose between two directions in my outer life actions; the other between two directions in my inner life emotions.

The outer life choice started with a stark, basic decision: to live or not to live. And for me, living meant finding a way to make Tariq's life and death meaningful. Those are the actions I have tried to take.

The emotional choice revolved largely around how I would process my feelings about Tony Hicks: my son's killer. My initial reaction was that he was a victim, too. But that didn't rule out the possibility that, at some point, I might come to see him in a terrible light: a victim, yes, but a villainous victim who took something precious and deserved my wrath.

I was once asked: if it were my decision, where would Tony be today? This is a very tough question. A wrenching question. I do think there is a certain amount of punishment he has to go through. And he is.

But in the previous chapter, I pointed out that relentless anger, or hatred, or lust for revenge, can corrode our insides like a virulent acid. I thank God that is not the path I took. With three years' perspective behind me, I can now name the path I am on regarding young Tony Hicks.

It is a path called forgiveness.

In her book, *The Thirst for Wholeness*, Christina Grof brings out many of the key characteristics of the incredibly complex act we call forgiveness. One of them explains why I say I can name the path I am on, not the destination I have arrived at:

> *Forgiveness is not a complete, permanent act. It is not something that occurs at one moment in time. It is not a line we step over; on one side, we have not yet forgiven, and on the other, we have thoroughly forgiven, forever. Forgiveness is not an event, it is a process.*

That distinction between "event" and "process" captures something important. There may be an end point—but not necessarily. In real life, some journeys don't end.

Grof also points out that forgiveness doesn't work well as a form of denial, or a protective barrier against hurts still living in us. It's not going to magically anesthetize the underlying pain one has suffered.

It can't be forced. It may not even be volitional at all. It's not necessarily for the benefit of the forgiven one. *Forgiveness occurs when preparation meets grace,* she says. In other words, when an inner voice of truth says it's time to let go, and it's good to let go, and our spirit is ready to hear that voice, it becomes possible to let go. And that release can do wonderful things for us. That it may also do wonderful things for the forgiven one is, in a sense, a spiritual bonus.

No, I haven't gotten over the loss of Tariq. I never will. But in my heart—at least as far down as I can drill—I have given Tony, the victim at the other end of the gun, my personal absolution.

And what is equally meaningful is that he asked for that. I believe he wanted and needed that, very deeply.

Forgiveness has been asked for and given. And I have reached an important point. I'm ready to do something I've been turning over in my mind for a long time.

I'm ready to meet Tony Hicks.

You see, despite my intellectual understanding of his victimhood, the compassion for his circumstances, my desire to see him restored, and the spiritual acknowledgment of his soul, there's no denying it: his is the brain that decided to shoot; his is the finger that pulled the trigger. Until now, I don't think I could have stood the emotional firestorm of being face to face with Tony, or even being in the same room with him. That's one of the reasons I'm grateful a trial wasn't necessary.

But I think I'm ready now. I'll make an even stronger statement. I think it's *right* now. It's the final step toward healing.

Not too long ago, I had dinner with Ples. I told him we need to start thinking about my meeting Tony. And oh, what a difficult meeting that's going to be. For both of us. But it needs to happen. For both of us.

And when I do travel to the facility where Tony serves his sentence, and when at last Tariq's father and Tariq's killer are face to face, here's what I'll tell him:

I'll tell him I want him to have hope.

I'll tell him that my dream is to have our healing stride side by side in partnership and trust.

I'll tell him that his plea, his sentencing statement, his videotape, his letter to his classmates, have been meaningful actions of personal responsibility and restoration.

I'll tell him that we both learned the same lesson at the hand of the same great teacher, human pain: *violence destroys us.*

I'll tell him of my belief that we share the same desire: to shield other children from the pain of that lesson.

I'll tell him that our souls—his, Tariq's, mine, Ples', all of ours—will be together again. Next time, the circumstances will be happier.

And finally, I'll tell him that when he is released, I want him to come to work at the Tariq Khamisa Foundation. I want him to complete our restoration by being a living, working witness to the power of restoration. I *know* he can convince children to think things through at critical times; to make right choices, not violent choices. He'll have been through so much. His voice will carry the truth and impact that can only come from one who's been there. When he uses that voice, he'll help restore his community.

By working as a force for good in Tariq's name, I want him to meet Tariq again. And this time, rather than meeting in a street of death and grief, I want them to bond: the soul of one departed and the soul of one still here, moving together in harmony and righteousness.

When that happens, my journey from murder to forgiveness will be complete.

Afterword

New Year's Day, 1995, arrived with optimism and promise. I looked forward to a good year for myself and my grandson, Tony. In the five years he had been living with me, I had committed myself to being the best parent I could be to him. I thought I had provided all of the love, guidance and support any troubled young person could need.

Twenty-one days into the year the optimism and promise vanished like morning mist in the sun's heat. My loving grandson, 14 years old, had committed murder.

It is difficult to express the depth of the grief I felt for the family whose son was slain on that tragic evening. It is even harder to convey the horror, guilt and unabated sadness my family and I felt for my grandson.

The knowledge that my grandson had brought death to one of God's children, and torment to his victim's loved ones, compelled my prayers and propelled me to my faith. I needed to do everything I could to comfort Tariq's family and mine. I desperately needed to figure out what would be right, what would be healing.

Then Azim Khamisa reached out his hand to me. It was a gesture of friendship—and much more. It said, "We both carry a burden of loss. Help me carry mine. Let me help you carry yours." I was invited to join him in the struggle to right the wrongs which had cost us both so dearly. When I took that outstretched hand, I knew I had found my path to healing.

Many people have asked, "How can this be? How can the father of the victim and the grandfather of the perpetrator join their hands together?" I believe it is because Azim Khamisa and I both see ourselves as God's children. I was imbued with a great love for Azim from the moment I saw his heart revealed through his actions. Though shrouded in grief, he did not seek revenge. He sought to better a society in which a young child could possess a handgun and use it to kill.

I was raised in the working-class poor neighborhoods of south Los Angeles. My upbringing taught me to be wary. When I looked at people, it was easier to see badness than goodness. In times of stress and trauma, it may be easier for all of us to see bad than good. But Azim Khamisa's response to the murder of his son—as stressful and traumatic an event as most of us are ever likely to face—will stand forever as an example of the profound goodness within us.

The legal process has taken its course; justice has been served. My grandson took his first step toward redemption by pleading guilty and taking responsibility for his crime. He has sought forgiveness from those he has harmed. While serving his lengthy prison term, he has pledged to work hard to be a better person.

I communicate with Tony by mail and periodic visits. I still try to provide the love, guidance, support and encouragement I was committed to before our lives changed so traumatically. The parenting goes on, to the best of my ability, even through steel bars.

My daughter may never recover from the emotional shock of the crime committed by her son, and his imprisonment. But she is working to overcome her depression. She is strongly committed to Tony, to the successful completion of his sentence and his return to society. She and I continue to seek God's guidance and strength in our efforts to support Tony, the Khamisa family, and each other.

Three years have passed since that terrible night. And from the sorrow, like a phoenix from its desert ashes, new hope has risen. The Tariq Khamisa Foundation will educate children early and continually on the consequences of violence. They will be given tools for breaking the deadly cycle, for rethinking life situations. The Violence Impact Forums have been tried, tested and proven to positively affect attitudes and behavior. It is clear to parents, teachers, counselors—and the children—that the VIF approach can work. We're on the right track.

And we need to be. All across our country, communities are faced with troubling problems that may be precursors of youth violence. Have you noticed that sometimes it seems easier for our children to hate than to love? Easier for them to lie than to speak the truth? Easier for them to play the "gangster" role than the "hero" role? These are alarm bells, and we're all responsible for answering them.

Azim's journey is a testament to the power of forgiveness. Through that power, we both rose up from the devastation that struck us down. We are united in trying to save other families from the lightning strike of senseless violence. As I look at what we are doing together, and what we can accomplish together, I look inside myself, and find again the seeds of optimism and promise.

Ples W. Felix, Jr.
February 1998

Afterword

Epilogue

Two days after Tariq was killed, the neighbors on Louisiana Street created a street shrine for him. He didn't live in that neighborhood—but the people who did were horrified and saddened that he had died there. They wanted to commemorate him. I don't know whose idea it was. Maybe it wasn't any one person's idea.

They placed flowers, mementos, prose and poems on the shrine. While I was standing there with Tasreen, Almas, Dan, Jennifer and Nazir, a young boy approached the shrine. He said he had lost his brother six months ago in a motorcycle accident, and someone had given him a poem. Now he wanted to share the poem with us. He left it there, unsigned, handwritten on a plain sheet of lined, yellow paper. I have not been able to find the original author's name, but this poem whispers deep within my heart:

> *Do not stand on my grave and weep*
> *I am not there*
> *I do not sleep*
> *I am the one thousand winds that blow*
> *I am the diamond glints of snow*

Azim's Bardo

I am the SUNLIGHT on ripened grain
   I am the gentle Autumn rain

When you awaken in the morning
Hush,
   I am the swift uplifting rush
Of quiet birds in circling
       flight
I am the soft stars that shine at night

Do not stand on my grave and
     cry
I am not there, I did not
    die.